Toepicks, Cadaver Dogs, and Sports with No Balls

Sherry Bosley

Toepicks, Cadaver Dogs, and Sports with No Balls

Wheat Field Press

Copyright © 2009
All Rights Reserved
*Toepicks, Cadaver Dogs,
and Sports with No Balls*
Sherry Bosley

Cover and book design:
Melaney Welch Moisan
Illustrations: Samantha Milio

Photos by Daphne Backman, Michelle Wojdyla, and the author.

Wheat Field Press
PO Box 20237
Keizer, OR 97307

ISBN 978-0-578-03193-4

Pilar Bosley and the Diamonds performing at Worlds

Table of Contents

Prologue | 1
1. Disposable Cash | 5
2. The Ball Game | 9
3. I Fell Off the Trapeze | 13
4. First Blood | 17
5. Practical Magic | 21
6. Two Bits | 25
7. Bunko League | 29
8. French Lesson | 33
9. Bunny Ears | 37
10. Precious Medals | 39
11. Deductive Reasoning | 41
12. Cadaver Dogs | 45
13. January Blahs, Cheese Balls, and Whirling Dildos | 49
14. Ugly Elves | 53
15. Opposites Attract | 57
16. Logic | 59
17. Park It | 63
18. Barking Up the Wrong Tree | 67
19. Bright Lights | 71
20. Temperatures Rising | 75
21. Princess and the P | 79
22. Recycle | 83
23. Trump Card | 87
24. Color Forms | 91
25. Ex-Wives | 95
26. Cropping Out | 97
27. The Kween | 99
28. Selling for Beans | 103
29. Numbers Game | 107
30. My Space | 109

31. Fruit of My Labor | **113**
32. Family Matters | **117**
33. Will Work for Shoes | **121**
34. Mother's Day | **125**
35. Bedazzled Canucks | **129**
36. Second Sunday in May | **133**
37. Getting the Time of Day | **137**
38. Three Questions | **141**
39. Stretching Fiction | **143**
40. Tree of a Thousand Suns | **147**
41. Running Circles | **151**
42. Conservative Estimate | **155**
43. When Worlds Collide | **159**
44. Coloring Between the Lines | **163**
45. Coat Closet | **167**
46. Writing the Wrongs | **171**
47. Traveling Band | **175**
48. Swapping Stories | **179**
49. Falling for It | **183**
50. Mousey Disposition | **187**
51. Photo Op | **191**
52. Security Deposits | **195**
53. Terrible Threes | **199**
54. Spinning | **203**
55. Common Scents | **207**
56. Gifts that Keep on Giving | **211**
57. Treating for Tricks | **215**
58. Coming Out of the Closet | **219**
59. Slip-Sliding Away | **2223**
60. Driving Force | **227**
61. It Must Have Balls | **231**
62. If I Were A Man, Or Beyonce's Upgrade | **235**

Acknowledgements | **241**

Author's Bio | **243**

PROLOGUE

As a writer, I tend not to like putting mere Xs in blocks.

I want to explain where, often, no explanation is wanted.

For example, on our income tax form I do not like to be relegated to "spouse," although I am a relatively happily married woman. I also do not like that I am forced to pick one title for occupation; it isn't that simple. I was a state trooper for fifteen years, and that is something you don't really leave behind. I am also an AKC dog show judge, although some think that is a mere hobby until they read the requirements to be licensed as such. I am currently a high school English Teacher, with a certification in Administration. And I am a writer.

But most importantly, surely vying for an equal title to spouse, is that of "mother." It is, after all, what shadows every decision I make. It has taught me how to make the really good cookies with the designs in the middle, and the importance of a will (literally and figuratively).

My children were planned and not the result of an accident. My husband and I adopted them from Korea. My daughter came home on January 9, 1989, when she was four months old. It is true I gave my Korean daughter a Spanish name, Pilar, without much thought to her sitting in kindergarten, with the teacher looking at anyone but the little Asian girl as she called out her name. Our son joined us in May of 1991, when he was eighteen months old.

What followed is what happens to writers, policewomen, teachers, dog show judges, and other moms as they traverse the choice of paths that lead from their lives.

In the winter of 1995, I saw an ad in the local newspaper for "Group Lessons" at the new ice rink in town. Although my children were only seven and six, they had exhausted every sport at the introductory phase. Soccer seemed pointless as every kid chased the ball. The turmoil of what seemed like 74 legs swatting a black and white globe lost its appeal after the first time-out. T-Ball was not exciting because, let's face it, the batting helmets always smelled like feet and old bubblegum. Gymnastics was entertaining, but again, there is quite a bit of standing around and flexing for a two-second experience on the mat.

I was quite resigned to responding when asked, "What do your kids do?" to saying "Coloring! They are both expert colorers. They rarely go out of the lines, and they have a steady stroke pattern." Let's be honest here, the requirement that children "be" or "do" something at an early age is more demanding than getting an Ivy League acceptance letter ten years later. And as a parent, it is your responsibility to connect your child with the right "do."

Still, I entered the ice-rink with a bit of trepidation. The summer recreation brochure had just come out, and I realized I was months away from shuttlecocks and croquet mallets unless there was a miracle on the ice.

My kids joined the other groups of winter-swaddled children on the far side of the rink, while the moms sat on cold metal bleachers cuddling cooling cups of coffee.

The miracle occurred.

My kids slid, coasted, air-planed, and scooted across the white surface without falling while their peers wiped-out in eye-averting calamities.

Later, in the lobby, a new experience befell the three of us. Moms gave me the evil eye while their offspring gathered near my duo in awe. The fact that their short statures easily prohibited their roll-over tendencies seemed to be overlooked in the process.

In the weeks that followed, even I noticed they picked up their edges and stops and cross-overs at an Evelyn Wood pace. Although equal in skills, Adam seemed more interested in the pattern of ice shaving he made when he practiced toe stops while Pilar was more focused on body position and blade edge.

It was inevitable that I would be approached by a coach, uttering the words, "Your daughter is very talented, she should take private lessons."

What followed has seemed at times to be a blessing and at other times several levels of hell that Dante left out of the final manuscript. Pilar progressed through training that eventually placed her as a national and international medalist, three years as USA Team member for the United States Figure Skating Association, and a training schedule that had a daily commute of 150 miles round trip.

Adam decided to give up frozen water and take to the pool and trained at Michael Phelp's NBAC and other pools for the corresponding years, truly offering me the choice of "when hell freezes over" and when it doesn't.

Disposable Cash

This is the time of year that I dread the most.

There are many reasons for this, but I have to be candid and admit that taking our taxes to the accountant is more daunting than going to Victoria Secret's to be measured for a bra.

On paper it looks like my husband and I are doing quite well — I mean it looks like we could be eating name brand canned green beans instead of the Safeway label. It suggests that we could own a condo at the beach instead of renting one for a week; one might assume we could have a vintage roadster in the garage instead of several boxes of old Christmas decorations.

After the second year, our accountant finally asked us, "What are you doing with your disposable cash?"

He admitted he had clients who gambled, and some who had a passion for Glen Fiddich and drank their bonuses shot glass by shot glass, and a few who speculated in unorthodox commodities.

We toyed with the idea of telling him we converted our cash into Japanese gold and hid it in the basement or that we had invested in a Koi farm, but we finally just admitted, "Our daughter skates."

"Oh," he said, rather surprised. Perhaps because as parents we do not look like ones that might produce an athletic prodigy; more likely, perhaps, we resemble a duo who might offer the world a child who would grow up to conjure up a better potato chip recipe.

"Like roller derby? I've heard that's making a come-back."

"No, as in ice skates," I reply.

My husband had gone into mute mode, as if this is something he would add to his list of improbable things, like the time I made him go to a couples baby shower or to a dog show in Orlando, or the lowest point: a Longaberger basket bingo.

"Oh, that's excellent—I understand that Michelle Kwan is a multimillionaire."

"Yes, well, our daughter ice dances." I don't elaborate, but perhaps my tone gives him a clue that this might be the equivalent of Vanilla Ice making a comeback in rap music.

"So, no return on the investment?" he queried softly.

My husband had started examining the wall art, which appeared to be several charcoal and ink sketches and a signed Artist's Proof. I did notice that the muscle above his right cheek was vibrating just a bit.

"Well," I began with some noticeable hesitation, "She did earn $3,500.00 this year from skating."

"And what was the outlay of expenses for this?"

I write a figure in pencil and slide the paper across the table to his waiting hand. He takes a deep breath and holds it before expelling it slowing. He has, of course, turned pale.

"I'm sorry," he says with such sincerity that I suspect he would be in Hallmark the next day looking for a card, if such a card existed.

"You realize ..." he starts, but I stop him.

"We know. But, of course, I'm sure you realize, not everything in life has a monetary value. My daughter is learning some very valuable lessons in life; she is learning self-discipline, and she gets to travel, and she seems to have a maturity level beyond her years."

I would have continued, but I see that he is also getting a twitch under his right eye similar to my husband's.

I don't know why they take it this hard; I mean what better way to eliminate cash flow than paying for skating. Hence, the appropriate term "disposable cash."

The Ball Game

Teaching high school seniors is daunting in any month of the calendar, but none quite compare to the last 30 days before graduation.

By then they have grown bored with my skating analogies (as in Everything in Life can be Learned in an Ice Rink), they are imagining summer days of sleeping past noon and evening hours without curfews and homework. They do not want to face the cold hard facts of life.

Take for example the class discussion that ensued after a recent reading of a pop culture essay regarding "Equal Rights."

"Why do we have to read about this All of The Time," one of my 12th-grade girls queried. "It was Back in the Day when people didn't get paid the same; you can't do that now."

"Really?" I replied, "Is this by law or moral compass?"

"You can be fined if you don't treat people equally. Everyone knows that," was the universal answer.

"Well, tell me what year it was Back in the Day when this all changed. That is your homework for the night."

The next day, of course, they arrived puzzled and perplexed.

"The Equal Rights Amendment has never been ratified—it fails to get enough states each time to back it," they proffered.

"But everyone just does it anyway because it is the right thing to do."

I sighed, because I felt like I was debunking their belief in Santa Claus and the Easter Bunny in one quick swoop.

"So there is equality in the workplace, not by law so much as by doing what is right. But not in sports, since men are obviously better."

This was of course brought forth a deluge of disagreement by the girls; the boys merely nodded in placid agreement.

"Girls can be equally talented in ANY sport," was the feminine battle cry.

The male naysayers pointed out the women could not dominate on the football field against "men," nor could most do pull-ups from a standard drop position.

The girls countered that boys are not typically gifted in artistic programs in gymnastics or cheerleading.

And then the civilities ended.

"We're talking about Real Sports," replied those in possession of Adam's apples. "We're talking about sports that have balls!"

This is where our moral compass fails, of course. This is where the gloves come off.

What is discovered in a classroom of 18-year-olds is just a microcosm of what is played out in our country everyday.

If you research any highest-paid-athletes list, you will discover that equality in sports rivals former Dark Ages practices regarding equality of the sexes. *Forbe's* Top Fifty Athletes (by salary) has nary a feminine moniker. The Top Paid "Action" Sports list (this a list of snowboarders, surfers, BMXers, and skateboarders, instead of GI Joes and Power Rangers as implied) also is without a bra-wearing athlete.

This has to be shocking considering the purses won and the endorsement deals garnered by Maria Sharapova, Annika Sorenstan, and the Williams sisters, and the dominance of these high earners in tennis and golf, sports that, in fact, require balls to be set in motion.

It is not a surprise then to discover that the event most viewed by the televised audience, and the highest priced ticket at any past Olympics — the Ladies Free Skate — has not produced an athlete who can join the ranks of Tiger Woods, Dave Beckham, Phil Mickelson, or Kimi Raikkonen (Formula One racing). Ice skating's (Is this in fact an "Action" sport?) greatest female athletes — Michelle Kwan, Kristi Yamaguchi, Peggy Fleming, and Dorothy Hamill (to name a few) — did not even get to hang on the lowest bar of that ladder of success.

In a time of bailouts and foreclosures, we are not sure how our laws are protecting us, or if they even exist.

Perhaps it is a sign of salvation and hope that so many have maintained and kept their own moral compasses pointed in the right direction.

Perhaps it is best we put aside forever this concept of what needs balls and what doesn't as a measure used to establish equality.

I Fell Off the Trapeze

When you have a sport injury, it's an automatic "thumbs up," red, white, and blue badge of courage.

It doesn't even matter how you got it.

It can be anything from "I caught an edge in the middle of a combination spin and flew into the boards" to " ... and the bike went off the mountain and landed in a 50-foot spruce tree" to "I got this nasty blood blister opening the sealed pack on a new can of tennis balls."

You get respect. You get a head nod. You get "That's rough but you were going for the burn" noise that starts in the back part of the throat of your consoler and can often be mistaken as the sound of one recovering from bronchitis by the uninformed.

If you get an injury that is not in some way connected to thinking about a sport, preparing to "sport," or actively being engaged in a sport, you get no consolation; you get no "Ahh, Man!" or claps on the back.

You get a frown.

Here is the truth: people want a story, and they want a good story. We have been brainwashed with the calamities of the wide world of sports and we can no longer accept that man walks on a sidewalk, man falls off the edge of the sidewalk; we have to have a competitive pursuit attached to it. Man had better have been preparing for his last round of Extreme Hop-

Scotch if he is going to fall off the sidewalk.

I have had plenty of injuries that earned gold stars; remember, I have been a trooper and a dog show judge. I can relate (by the method of six degrees) any bruise or scab to "It all started with a man with a gun" or "And then the 180-pound Rottie turned to stare me in the eye as I prepared to examine his reproductive equipment."

Most people wince by the second word, and I get the back clap, phlegm noise instantly.

But now, a not-so-funny thing has happened. I am entering the tunnel I believe my mother used to talk about. It is that tunnel that started with, "Wait until you have children of your own," and I guess somewhere in the middle is the "wait until you get older and your body starts to fall apart" mile marker.

I am limping around school and home, dreaming of a "Jazzy chair" or wheeled walker because of, as I have learned to classify it, a "gymnastics" injury.

Let me explain. I (wearing my earphones and listening to Bon Jovi) was performing the floor mat portion of my program, where I balanced on one knee, second leg extended in perfect toe point to the ceiling, as I tried to retrieve the document box from under our bed (this to verify that my passport doesn't expire this year). At some point, the degree of difficulty for this maneuver became apparent, and I lost an edge of my rounded patella and collapsed on my side clutching my international identity in my upraised hands moaning, "Why Me?"

After several minutes, I realized the medics were not going to come onto the field, only the standard poodle, with his oversized tongue, and the fox terrier, who saw no reason I could not throw her wubba, even if I was seeing stars and making odd noises that are typically reserved for trying on jeans from four summers past.

The pain did not stop when in the upright position. Nor did it stop in the sitting position.

When I walked, I limped and hobbled like a creature of Mary Shelley's fantasy.

I went to work, limping and battered, to be heralded by questions and bland stares at my answer.

"What? You were looking under your bed," they repeated in disbelief with extended frowns. "What were you doing?"

"I was on one knee, reaching under the bed, when I fell over in agony and despair," I finally retorted to the fifth person who raised an inquisitive eyebrow, "much like a beached harbor porpoise."

The doctor's receptionist finally cleared it all up for me. "The sport's medicine doctor can see you on Tuesday. He is really double-booked this entire week."

"Can't I see my regular doctor tomorrow?" I persisted.

"Well, you could, but that would be a waste of time, since she would refer you to the Sport's Med section and then you would be a few days later getting in."

"But, I wasn't playing sports. I was ... " I pause confessionally, "I was merely kneeling, and I mean it was on only one knee, but still ... "

"Exactly, and so you must see our Sport's Medicine doctor, just as I said."

So, I have another twenty-four hours until I can see the guru of the fit and fittest. But I have learned from my mistake.

Now when I am asked "What happened to your leg," I pause for a moment and look out into the distance.

"I knew it was going to be a difficult maneuver, but I was determined to give it my all. Any possibility for international travel depended on it. When my music came on, I took my starting position and went down on one knee. I was so in the moment I didn't even realize what had happened until the pain blocked out all conscience thought."

Now that I think about it, Extreme Hop-Scotch might just have some merit as a real league.

Sherry Bosley | 15

First Blood

So here is the thing about being a mom, and then a skating mom: I have been told I am a bit "intense." To be honest, this may be an accurate assessment. But the skating part is coincidence, not causation.

I think I am a little bit like Sylvester Stallone, as in *First Blood*, not *Rocky I-V*. (Please, I could never do all those steps!) I am basically a calm and centered person until someone takes the first swipe, and then I get all bandana-tied-around-the-forehead action figure — at least this is how I imagine it.

In reality there have only been a few times I have felt my eye start to twitch in the skating arena. Typically these were times when the technical caller made a few miscalculations in spin revolutions or blade-to-head awareness, or when someone thought my daughter's new free dance was (gasp) "off the rack." And then there's the one time I overheard a newbie say, "She needs to work on expression," and verified this was not a family affliction.

So, I think you can agree with me that being "intense" has just as many positive connotations as negative. Perhaps, even more.

People come to expect things from you. You become the "go to girl." You take care of business.

Some uninformed people have relegated this to "overreacting," which of course is ridiculous. I just pull out all the stops to get whatever job needs to be done — well — done.

To do this, I have taken on many personas. I have had helicopters looking for lost dogs. I have gone through the retired LAPD to obtain a back-stage pass to see Michelle Kwan for my daughter. I have booked airline tickets that take different routes to guarantee arrival in bad weather for Junior Nationals.

So, no one should be surprised when I "took action" after my daughter called me this morning and told me someone had "double-keyed" her car.

"Did this happen at the rink or at your apartment?" I asked in my Miss Marple voice.

"I don't know. I think at my apartment. It was dark when I left the rink last night, but I would have seen this; it is very noticeable.

I discounted her observation; she lives three blocks from the rink so the list of suspects would be practically the same at either location.

"Mom, I don't want you to do anything. I'll call the police and make a report. There is no reason to be alarmed."

"Sure, dear. That's fine." Of course I knew that she knew this would not be the case. Within an hour I had her apartment manager agree to install security cameras in the back of the building, the chief of police agree to conduct drive by surveillances, and called in a few favors from my former days as a state trooper.

At six o'clock the phone rang.

"Mom, you didn't call anyone did you"?

"Define anyone?"

"Mom! There's a man outside in camo gear standing about 10 feet from my car."

"Really, look again, there should be two."

"MOM!"

"I think you need to consider how crazy some people are in this world. You need to be cautious."

"I am aware there are crazy people in the world. Very aware."

I pretended not to hear the sarcasm dripping from her voice.

"Good. Now, you need to double click your door locks before getting in your car in the morning. There are motion detectors installed in the quarter panels."

"Mom, I really hate it when you get like this."

"Sorry, dear, I didn't hear you, my bandana slipped over my ears."

Pilar Bosley in costume for an Emerald Theatre-on-Ice performance

Practical Magic

We are sitting in the middle of a winter snowstorm that has blanketed the east coast with a five- to ten-inch accumulation. Schools are closed, government offices are in code red, which seems to translate to "if you are crazy, come on in to answer the calls as you'll be the only one here." Yes, most people with any time available are calling in to take personal days.

My daughter called to tell me that her college is closed, but "the rink is open and I have to be there for a 5:00 lesson."

I look out the window that now appears to contain a total white-out in the frame, and with forty-mile-an-hour wind gusts, the snow is actually blowing vertically as if from some topsy-turvy snow globe.

She doesn't answer me, and I understand why.

It is our shameful secret, one I am sure will come out on Oprah, Ellen, or, God-forbid, Jerry Springer in some awful taping of "Athletes Raised Wild."

Skaters and their designated drivers never miss a day at the rink. And I feel the heads bobbing everywhere. There is an added wind gust outside my winter wonderland. I'm not talking about competitions; I'm talking about your every-day-I-have-practice-at-the-rink type day.

We have missed birthday parties, family reunions, cookouts, baptisms, and showers just so skates could be laced for one more day.

We have driven through snow, sleet, and hail; we have plowed through the remnants of a hurricane, kept a look-out in a tornado watch, and waded through a flood warning to make it to the rink on time.

We have driven with fevers, flus, and fears. We have ridden with blisters, blights, and blubbering. We have taken off work and off school. We have used vacation and holiday time. We have answered a 5:00 a.m. alarm clock, and walked in as the late night monologues began.

And all for "A Practice."

"Sweetie," I pause and lick my lips, which have suddenly gone dry and parched. "You can miss one lesson."

It is like when Harry Potter calls out the name "Lord Voldemort," and the others cringe at the very sound. I feel her intake of breath on the other end of the phone.

"It will be clear by 5:00," she offers hopefully.

I look out at the wind shear that now appears to be at 60 knots and hear the ice pellets pinging the storm door.

I shake my head although she can't see me.

"What if," I say, pausing to get courage, "what if you miss one day?"

With the words out, I search them for feasibility. I realize they will have the same effect as taking money from the collection plate at Sunday church or asking a dinner hostess for fresh coffee that does not taste like burnt toast.

We go to each practice with much the same mindset as we presumably buy lottery tickets. This might be the one, even though it is a long shot, this might be the one in a million, where it all lines up, and it all makes sense; the feet work with the brain, and the brain works with the coach.

Magic happens.

And we all want the magic. If we miss this one practice, on this one day, then we might miss the chance we have to find our magic.

"I'm sure it will clear up before I have to leave." My daughter answers as I knew she would.

"You're probably right." I say a little louder, so she'll be able to hear me over the wind howling down the flue in the fireplace.

"Make sure you leave a bit earlier so you have plenty of time."

"I always do! I have to stretch before I go on the ice."

I sigh and admit defeat. At least Ellen dances with her guests before she grills them.

Two Bits

As I am typically an optimistic person, it is hard to think in negatives, but occasionally we must. If I had a list of things I abhor doing, it would be topped with items like calling my health insurance company with any question that cannot be answered by the automated choice selections by pressing one through nine, going to any Motor Vehicle Administration building for any reason, especially to have a new driver's license photograph taken. And the third and final thing on my list is having a yard sale.

A yard sale, or tag sale as it is called in some parts of the country, is held when you realize that nothing else will fit on the shelves in the basement or garage. The premise is this: you offer your goods to the world at a fraction of their cost, and the world then counteroffers with, "Will you take a quarter for this?"

I actually love to go to yard sales, although I don't do it often. There is a hierarchy in the art of yard-saling. Consumers may judge the location of the event, and upscale addresses garner more traffic because everyone is hoping the owners are discarding a Chanel or some silver that has started to tarnish. The start time is another art form. Most yard sales start at 8 a.m., but hawkers start arriving as the moon settles on the horizon. Sometimes these professionals drive by slowly, scanning your goods with all the skill of a self-checkout register at

Home Depot. Sometimes they roll down the window and ask in a rough, Marlboro-soaked voice, "Got any scrap gold?"

This weekend my husband and I decided to hold a yard sale at my friend's house. She lives on a busy cut-through street that does not even require the posting of signs. This, of course, required the extra step of loading and unloading our plethora of cast-off treasures several times.

My husband had his usual collection of relic gardening tools, boxes of screws, a carton of fifty ball caps he has collected through the years, and some golf "joke" gifts that included an exploding golf ball, a golf ball water globe, and a flask disguised as a golf club.

I had an offering of things I have given, but have not been well received. These included a tank top I had purchased for my daughter in Lake Placid seven weeks ago, a Transformer that doubled as an MP3 player, several Trolls still in the boxes purchased long after my daughter stopped liking them, which apparently had a window of opportunity of twenty-six minutes. I also had the usual glass vases and cutesy baskets that accompany delivered flower arrangements.

But I had some other items of interest. My husband placed two Rubbermaid containers on the ground and unveiled ten pair of used figure skates, size 6.5. It was a bit overwhelming. I could only compare it with bees: one bee can be annoying if buzzing your head or itchy if it actually stings you, but a swarm can be debilitating if they surround your body or a dozen decide to sting you.

I struggled for breath for a moment as I viewed their scuffed ivory leather tops and glistening silver blades. I would have asked for an EPI pen to avoid an attack if either of us used such a thing. How they haunted me, those twenty soles that together amassed more than 11,000 of my hard-earned dollars.

"What should we do with them?" I whispered.

"Sell them!" My husband responded.

I looked at him and wished I hadn't, since he was sporting one of the ball caps he had acquired who knows when and had thankfully been stored in a box for decades — a colorful Scooby-Doo missive in bright blue.

"How much should we ask for them?"

My husband scratched his head under the cap and said decisively, "Ten dollars."

Ten dollars? "I think companies get more in a tax sale. Isn't that like taking a penny for a dollar?'

Now my husband looked at me like I was wearing a hat that said, "Rouh-Ro." Right. I forgot that he liked to live in that world that is shared by many institutions, "Don't ask, don't tell" when it comes to all costs associated with figure skating.

As the day progressed, the tables started to empty. We would not be taking home the Trivial Pursuit and Battleship games or the box of old phones. Two of our old dog crates and exercise pens found a home with a woman who said she had rabbits and chickens.

The vat of Beanie Babies remained untouched, as did the tubs of skates.

A woman noticed my focus and said, "They do look beat-up don't they?"

My eye started twitching.

I wanted to explain what they had lived through; this pair had won a medal at Nationals, this pair had won Sectionals, and this pair had been to France, but I couldn't. I couldn't tell which pair was which.

Instead, I said, "There is still a lot of life left in them."

The woman nodded doubtfully and seemingly out of pity since she clearly wore a size ten, she said, "I'll give you a quarter for a pair."

Next summer I may ask the event chair if it will be possible to have one of those Decorate the Skate for Charity events to raise money for the Lake Placid Ice Dance Championships.

I have 20 skates I can donate.

Bunko League

I joined a Bunko group last year.
Oh, alright, I'll confess, I organized the whole thing. I did this as I do many things, wholeheartedly and with very little information. I didn't know what a Bunko was, or how to get one, but I liked the sound of it. Audibly, well, it sounds a little mysterious and perhaps on the edge of being illegal. What can I say, Nationals were over and the summer looked far away.

The premise is basically that an established group of woman meet each month at a different house. We sit at three (or four) tables of four and throw down three dice trying to get the most of each called number. You get a Bunko if you roll three dice with the called number. You get a Baby if you get three of same number of an uncalled digit.

The fun part is that after each called number, you rotate and sit at a different table with different people.

There is a cacophony of yelling and laughing and the stories keep us laughing into the next week. (Please! This week Kristien told us about using a stall in her work bathroom that had been converted to a handicap facility. To do this, they just took out the divider for one stall and put on a bigger door. The handicap stall still has two toilets in it, but it also has an oversized door. She was showing us her injured finger which she damaged when she slipped while jumping from one toilet to the other while using the facilities. I know, the visual of this will keep me going for a month). This also shows that it is important to select a core group of like-minded people.

We also do a great deal of eating. By this I mean we don't eat anything after breakfast, so we are prepared for the buffet. We usually spend the first hour eating before letting the dice leave our hand; in fact, we are convinced we can't roll the bones unless we have been stuffed.

Here's the thing: we are all competitive women.

Oh, we do it for the fun and fellowship, but we are also motivated by the food and prizes. (Oh yes, there are four great prizes for the evening, so your odds of winning with a little bit of Lady Luck are good.) The hostess selects the prizes each month and then collects the $5 fee per lady as reimbursement.

I was the hostess of the first Bunko in February, and I bought books: Oprah's selection for a previous month and one of my favorite Elizabeth Peter's mysteries, as well as a Longaberger basket for the prizes. I had a beautiful bounty of offerings in the kitchen that ranged from crab dip to homemade (okay, maybe it was just the sauce) meatballs. I had a plethora of delectable cookies and cakes for snacking.

Now let me skip ahead to our most recent Bunko, this past Friday. The hostess lives in a beautiful home that had been professionally cleaned that day. (She also has no pets so at no time during the night did little cat or dog hair dust balls float out from under the center island). She used some old family recipe to create homemade meatballs in a delicate sauce. She baked individual Brie pastries with homemade jelly and fresh mint. She made chocolate cookies with freshly grated nuts and imported vanilla that didn't come from Costco. She baked miniature coconut cream pies that she swore she just "threw in the blender." She also had some dips and crackers and vegetables on the other side of the counter to satisfy everyone who was elbowed out while the main herd poked at the meatballs, cookies, and pies.

But here is the kicker. She then brought out these little cakes that were covered in peanut butter and chocolate that no one has the recipe for, except Tasty-Kake and this hostess.

By the fourth one, I was fuming.

How can we compete with this? What can I do for the next game night when it's held at my house? Have it catered by Paula Dean? Do I beg a Keebler Elf for a recipe? This has gotten way out of hand. No one will ever be able to serve a Lil Frank wrapped in a piece of Crescent roll again.

And the prizes! Well, it is the choice of the hostess, but I personally thought I was being considerate by not foisting off a piece of skating memorabilia, say a skate Christmas ornament, or a copy of Michelle Kwan's autobiography. Instead, I offered sources of literary history and a representative piece of iconic art by a family of basket weavers in the heartland.

This hostess has us vying for crystal and original art works (or so it seems) at our monthly league meeting. Soon we will need to register with Tiffany or Cartier.

I bring this up because I organized this group last February when skating was over for the year (somewhat), and I had a little time on my hands. I suggested it because we were all a competitive lot, and it is a good way to while away the hours before Lake Placid and after Nationals. It also gives you an opportunity to scream out loud, which is mandatory for the game and is something we stifle at other competitive events.

So, looking ahead as my turn as hostess nears once again, I am currently compiling recipes for hand rolling sushi, planning to have a banana pudding flown in from Paula's Georgian restaurant, and looking at swatches to have my living room chairs redone.

I'm still toying with the idea of those skate Christmas ornaments. If I can take them to Nationals and get them signed, they will become true collector items, awarded for the most Bunkos and most Babies for my February festive dice fiasco.

Top that Bunkoettes.

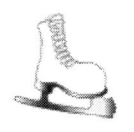

Pilar Bosley and John Corona performing to "Still Loving You" in their final performance for US Nationals

French Lesson

Sometimes you need to take a close look at your life, take stock, do an inventory. This could be at a milestone birthday, or just a benchmark you establish for yourself.

For me, it was getting my haircut.

Let me explain.

I am a product of the public school system, typically not a bad thing, but there are occasions when you have to wonder what the long term big picture is for the movers and the shapers of education. For example, in the 1970s the languages that were offered were Latin, French, and German. Spanish was not even on the table. Thirty years after the end of WWII, the fear that German dominance could resurge was so palatable that high school students were being pushed into classrooms where in reality the only society that *sprechen zie Deutsch* was, well, Germany.

After four levels of German, I am an adult who knows one phrase in the language: "Haben zie einen Fragen." I think this means something close to, "Do you have a question?" I believe this because Frau Mueller asked it of me everyday because of the look of puzzlement and confusion pasted on my face. The rest of my German knowledge comes from watching Hogan's Heroes and the four-minute scene in the "Sound of Music" where the Von Trapps make their escape under the noses of the German military. In addition to that, I have created my own hybrid German, which I guess is more like Pig-Latin German, where I cross reference two terms: "Geboyens," which I define as "The Boys" for when I call my dogs (this has no actual bearing on the fact that some are boys and some are girls) and telling my children that their "Fry-tag" (father) was home. They later learned this actually seems to mean Friday to most Germans, unless you are from the small clan that is located in the very, very west.

The point of this is, of course, I should have taken French. At least if I had taken French, I could have used it in life, unlike the aforementioned German, Algebra, and the Home Economics class that proffered a wearable dress at the conclusion of the class. If I had taken French, I could have read Victor Hugo's *Les Miserables* in the original language, ordered from a French menu with authority, and perhaps have had a passable accent when quoting Madeline or Pepe Le Pew.

It would have also come in handy at the hair salon my daughter sent me to, which not only has a French name, but also a French price-list: no amounts are posted.

In taking stock of my life, in the things I am not proficient in, I have to add to the foreign language deficit the fact that I am hair impaired. I have mentioned this before. Oh, I have plenty of hair, but I do not have the knack to twist it in hot rollers or wrap it around a brush that produces the coiffures I so envy. Adding product is also a mystery to me. No real measurements are given. "Add a dollop of mousse" to me imitates putting Redi-Whip on chocolate pudding: the more the better. This, however, typically results in my looking like I have just run in a marathon or been traveling in a standing position in a convertible across country.

My daughter suggested I go to a salon in her city.

"You should go to a stylist for your haircut and a colorist for your highlights. It's just like in skating, one coach gives you a program, the other works on your compulsories. Very few people can be experts in all fields."

Since we have been paying for this multi-coverage for

years, I could not argue with the logic. I made an appointment at the French-named salon in her town, paid $11.00 in tolls and gas for the 150-mile round trip, and arrived full of hope.

I was checked in, caped, and cappuccinoed in a matter of minutes by staff who were all bedecked in black pants, white crisp shirts, and black pointy shoes with a plethora of straps and buckles.

My stylist evaluated my hair with much lip pursing.

"Oh my!"

My colorist pushed through my crown like someone who has lost a diamond earring in the grass.

"Oh dear."

In two hours I sat in the chair and beheld a vision in the mirror: a great cut that had taken four hair products, three brushes, and twenty minutes of contortionist blow-drying to produce, and highlights stunning in their simplicity (or so I was told).

It was lovely, but just like speaking German, I knew I would not be able to reproduce the look after the first washing. I suspected I would look like Winona Ryder during her shop-lifting years whence I raised a brush and diffuser to my own head.

The conclusion of my visit was with, of course, the accounts agent and booking specialist.

"That will be $258.00 today. Would you like to set up your next appointment now?"

I stood with debit card poised at the marble counter and considered all the Rosetta Stone language boxes I could purchase with what would be my projected annual expenses at this salon.

"Did you want to leave a 20 percent tip per custom?"

Is that the custom in France, I thought? I had missed so much in pursuit of a dead-end language.

I merely nodded my head and a volumnized tress broke free of its mud-molded position behind my ear.

"Have a wonderful day," she said as she handed me back my card.

"Gutten Tag." I answered.

Bunny Ears

This past week has marked significant religious events for a huge percentage of the world population: Easter and Passover. These are in fact the most serious of all the annual causes for celebration and/or awareness in formalized religion.

So, it does seem a bit paganistic that the season is marked for some with the annual quest for the Holy Grail of the Spring Holiday: that's right, the quest for the best chocolate Easter Bunny.

And, let's be honest, we judge the elements of chocolate on a scale that might be compared to beloved sporting events: the technical qualities and the esthetics (PCS).

So, we could purchase the chocolate rabbits offered at the chain discount department stores. These are inexpensive, have a universal taste, but alas, they have no distinction. They are typically named Peter Rabbit or Bo Bunny, the chocolate is tasty, but it is almost translucent in places where the waxed surface was formed in very thin sections.

A step up from this is the luxury chocolates that are as mass-produced as the real rabbits in the wild.

The taste is richer, their smoothness has a solid feel, but something essential is still missing.

In high school I took, as most high school juniors still take, those career tests that supposedly align you with your dream vocation. But, let's be honest, they hold out on the best jobs.

No one told me when I was 16 that I could possibly aspire to become a Chocolatier. (I know, it sounds like the fifth member of the Three Musketeers).

And yet, it is with these magicians of liquid brown gold that we find the essence of perfection. It is in these small establishments that we find the perfect bunny or turtle or blue jay. Real artists rarely stick with what is traditional or expected.

Here there are no candy button eyes, mold lines, or blank expressions. Here we find the Mona Lisa of smiles forming the lips of a Rhinelander or Flemish Giant hare. Here, the velvet flavor melts only in your mouth after leaving no disfiguring fingerprints from the touch.

True sadness comes from breaking off the ears or leg for consumption, much like the sadness we feel at the end of a beautiful free dance; you want the moment to never end, but you are also aware you could not handle the heightened emotion of a prolonged interaction.

And so the body follows the ears and leg.

What is there about the chocolate form of an animal that so haunts us for the other eleven months of the year?

It is a passion that cannot be satisfied with chocolate covered peanuts, hearts, or candied corn at other holidays. We are, it seems, by nature, chocolate carnivores.

I was fortunate to find a brilliant chocolatier several years ago. He supplies me with fabulous animal artifacts in milk or white medium and even supplies me with a small baggie of broken pieces when I make my annual pilgrimage to his shop.

This year he crafted the finest Terrapin seen in captivity for my son and a Siamese Lop-Ear with an angelic face for my daughter. My daughter, very savvy, immediately packed her chocolate prize away, much like removing a human from the Cullen family. My son, on the other hand, told me he didn't want to take the turtle back to college, and he would leave it in the pantry until he comes home for summer break.

He went back to his fraternity last night, sans turtle.

For the record, I resisted for 49 hours.

Precious Medals

I am on subject overload.

After staying up for two weeks until the early hours of the morning to watch tumbling girls, breast-stroking guys, and repentant relay runners, I was content when the last firework dimmed in Beijing.

At last things could get back to normal.

Normal to me is feeling excitement when I notice gasoline is down to 3.38 a gallon; I parlay that with the fact that the opening and closing ceremonies for the Olympics had a 75 million dollar price tag. It is hard not to think of what else that money could have done. There were nations represented that live in utter poverty and a portion of that budget would have meant food and medical attention for many suffering souls.

It is hard not to imagine what that budget could do if applied to our own athletes. We had the highest medal count I believe — I really stopped checking the statistics by the second week — although most of the training of our talent is paid from the pockets of the parents or the athletes. I heard storyline after storyline of parents who had mortgaged homes and taken second jobs to pay for the pursuit of dreams. And there are thousands back home who didn't make the team. They may have been fourth, fifth, or twentieth, but they train just as hard, and it costs just as much.

And those of us in ice-dancing know some harsh facts.

This is not the most popular of all skating genres, and skating in and of itself is on a downslide for viewing audiences. What is clambered for are the "tougher" sports: BMX racing, the half-pipe that houses curling snowboards, skiers who flip and twist as they leap off of mountains.

And yet we stay, we parents who fund and support the skating dream. Skaters who rise at 5 a.m. to lay tracks on freshly cleaned ice. Skaters who continue skating and working off ice to condition and strengthen bodies for hours and hours on end.

Most people think it is about what we just witnessed: an Olympic dream.

But it rarely is, for it is rarely accomplished.

My daughter explained it to me several seasons ago, but I don't think I truly understood until just recently. She told me it was "just doing something that you truly love the best that you can do it."

How often do we get the chance to do that?

So, although I am on subject overload and have an image of Michael Phelp's chest supporting eight gold medals, and I must face the Democratic Convention and Republican Convention news coverage, I am not resorting to watching old episodes of "Friends" or "Sex in the City."

For the third time, I am rereading my all-time favorite novel.

Deductive Reasoning

It is that time of year that all citizens dread.
But, of course, skating parents walk with the slowest feet. That's right, "It is tax time."

Our accountant is a bit unusual in that he thinks he could be a stand-up comedian. I know this because he frequently gives you one-liners that only he finds amusing.

For example, he sits with his Pierre Cardin tie asunder and murmurs, "Your 40K is really a 401 AC for Austrian Crystals."

This year he decided we should establish our "net worth," as he had attended a conference that advised — because so many people were depressed this year — that it would be a public service for accountants to remind those down-in-the-dumpers to take stock of what they really do have and perhaps it isn't really such a gloomy situation.

Of course the flip side of that is that it might be worse.

My husband is the "glass is half empty" kind of personality," so we better save it in case we get *really* thirsty."

I am more of a "Wow, that's just about the right amount to have enough room to add something else" type.

Exactly! I am creative.

My husband handled the real estate, life insurance policies, retirement funds, depreciation schedules, and capital gains projections for the project, and I was dealt the task of finding "anything else."

Sherry Bosley | 41

I didn't think this was such a difficult assignment until we were sitting in the accountant's office and he started rubbing his forehead.

I had found a cadre of treasures to list under "Art."

"You have here 1988 Chanel bag at $2,000.00."

"Well, I thought it was better to undervalue it then to place a current market price on it. Things are not really going for what they used to in these times of economic woe."

"You're talking about a 20-year-old purse?"

"I know, it is extremely rare."

Mr. Bull looked at my husband, and my husband looked back at Mr. Bull.

"I think he is saying it doesn't count," my husband said quietly.

I raised my eyebrows at this. "You're saying a Chanel purse in perfect condition cannot be considered as an asset. It started as a piece of art and is still a piece of art. But, a 1964 Mercury Comet that sold for $2,250.00 new and was, well, common, is now valued at $8,000.00 and is an asset?

The men look at each other, and Mr. Bull accepted the gauntlet, "It has historic tags."

I shook my head at both of them. "It's a vintage bag!"

Mr. Bull shuffled to the next page and put on a pair of glasses that appeared to have plain lenses to me. He moved them up and back on his nose a few times before speaking.

"You have two Team USA jackets listed at $60,000.00 a piece."

I nodded, but saw he needed some additional explanation.

"Yes, that would be one current model and the jacket they had in the Olympic year, which frankly was not as attractive or made as well."

"But they didn't cost that much money. That was what was given out as a reward."

"Oh no, they most certainly did cost that much money. There was no way to get one without spending that much money on everything: coaching, ice time, costumes, choreography, travel ..."

"But no one would spend that much simply to buy a jacket. Just the jacket."

"I beg to differ. Four years ago they medaled at Nationals and still did not make the team, and they were listed as substitutes for the entire international season. Substitutes don't get jackets. I would have gladly written a check for $60,000.00 that year to get the jacket."

"But you didn't."

"No, but I wrote checks the following years, and they have jackets."

"But it wasn't for the jackets."

"I assure you it most certainly was FOR the jackets and what comes with it."

"Is this now your 401J plan, for jackets?" Even he could only bring up a small chuckle at this.

"If you need testimonials, I could have several hundred notarized statements here within three days from skating parents from all over the country."

"That's frightening."

"I know. I guess Fed-Ex Express is putting a crimp in the postal service if they're thinking of cutting back to five days."

Cadaver Dogs

With Nationals in the rearview mirror and Worlds a new moon away, my friend Karen and I ventured to New York City this week for the second oldest sports competition in our country, The Westminster Dog Show. (The oldest competitive event is The Kentucky Derby.) Since this event doesn't involve the use of balls, my husband was more than content to stay home and take care of Eliot and Izzy, our own dogs.

Since our disposable income is a luxury of the past, I took the advice of William Shattner and booked a hotel on Priceline.com. The premise of this service is that you decide what star rating you want in a hotel, you "bid" a price, and give them your credit card number. It is only after the fact that you find out the name of the hotel, and there are no cancellation provisions, although the former Captain Kirk fails to mention this. I selected a four-star hotel, because in New York City anything below this might land you in an establishment with 25-thread-count sheets and someone knocking on your door every hour for a changing of the guard so to speak.

Those with a suspicious mind might have been a bit skeptical when my bid of $150.00 a night was accepted by what turned out to be the main hotel for the dog show.

"Shouldn't those rooms be sold out?" Karen asked on the train ride north.

"Maybe there was a cancellation and we got in under the

Sherry Bosley | 45

wire," I proposed in my naïve, the-glass-is-three-quarter-full wisdom

If Victorian foreshadowing were being noted from our adventure, it would have started when we checked in.

"Oh," said Jason, the friendly front desk clerk, "I see we only have one room available, your room, and it has a king-size bed. (This, of course, turns out to be a coastal perspective type of thing; a Californian king is actually larger than a traditional king-size bed, and a New York king is actually a queen-size bed in rest of the world.)

"But Priceline guarantees two double beds?" I queried in reply.

Jason looked at me with what must have been a Basset Hound impersonation, obviously practiced and brought forth for the dog show, and said, "That's our last room. I can try to move you if something else becomes available."

I was beginning to realize why Mr. Spock had some issues with Captain Kirk, as I was left with no alternative: take the king (queen) or pay for a room I wouldn't be staying in and find another hotel and pay again, although at New York prices.

"That will be fine," I told Jason resolutely.

Karen and I waded through Bloodhounds and Mastiffs, crates, and buckets to get to the elevators. Westminster attracts entries from all over the United States, and some of the canine travelers had not had uneventful trips. By the smell of some of the crates, we could have subsidized our trip if we had thought to set up a stand selling doses of Imodium AD.

We got off the express elevator at the 18th floor and felt like we were in one of those Verizon commercials featuring a Dead Zone. Literally.

The floor seemed deserted except for two Ionic fans that were plugged in outlets down one of the corridors. Our corridor.

It is really hard to describe what we encountered. The closest I can come is those Stargate episodes where the characters go through an invisible portal, yet you can actually see it — it's fuzzy and filmy and you have to push your way through.

The smell hit us hard. We opened our mouths to ask, "What is ..." and then slammed them shut again as the smell entered the opening and paralyzed our vocal cords.

We sprinted to room 1806, threw open the door, and then slammed it against the stench that leaked in.

Karen opened the kitchenette window to get out any strays as I called down to Jason on the room phone.

"Is the bed too small?" he asked.

I looked at the 60-by-80 mattress and shook my head. I took a chance and took in some new air.

"No." I gasped. "The bed is fine. But what is that smell in the hallway. No offense, but all those dogs in the lobby that seemed to have eaten tacos or chimichangas for breakfast could bottle that aroma and sell it for perfume compared to this."

"Oh." Jason paused, and I could tell he was probably a Wharton graduate, who majored in Downplaying a Problem. "Is that still there?"

"Hasn't anyone else complained?"

"Well, they did."

I waited.

"We have several long-term renters on that floor, and we aren't allowed to go into those rooms during their lease."

"Have you seen them lately? Alive, I mean? How are the other people on the floor coping with the smell?

"Well, we've temporarily reserved that corridor for Priceline customers."

"And how are they coping?"

"This is the first complaint I've had about it from them."

"And how many Priceline people are here?"

"Counting you and your friend?"

"Yes. Counting Karen and myself."

"That would be, let me see, ah ... two. There would be two."

I sighed and looked at Karen who was lighting a cigarette in our nonsmoking room. The burning tobacco smelled honey

Sherry Bosley | 47

sweet. She started laughing and shaking her head.

"This is our life," she mouthed to me between a puff and a snort of mirth.

"Is there anything else I can help you with?" Jason asked on the other end of the line, and even I had to roll my eyes at this hyperbole.

"Yes, Jason. If someone checks in with a cadaver sniffing dog, could you send them up to our hallway?"

"I'll let you know if one becomes available, ma'am."

January Blahs, Cheese Balls, and Whirling Dildos

After a three-week break for the Christmas holiday festivities, it was not surprising that the bleak January doldrums would find me attending a Tastefully Simple food gathering and discovering (Surprise!) that it was also a home sex toy party. In addition to passing around the graham cracker crusted cheese ball, other things would be passed along that lit up, vibrated, and whirled like butterflies.

January had also brought on my children's reactions to my recently acquired Facebook account: ("That's just weird" and "I'm not being your friend!"). It seems that Facebook, which initially plotted their conception with a college crowd in mind, is now seeing the largest increase of new users not from the Hannah Montana set, but from those who know the words her father penned for "Ackey Breaky Heart.' That's right. Women over the age of 30 are joining by the millions to keep in touch with their friends who are scattering the globe in these strange economic times.

But, the most interesting event of the New Year was that it also delivered a ER visit due to chest pains that may or may not have been related to eating Mexican food for two days straight in my annual purification ritual from turkey, stuffing, and apple pie.

I find it odd that they ask you questions without establishing a baseline; for example, they ask you to "rate the pain on a scale of 1 to 10 with 10 being the most pain you have ever experienced. I mean, really, they should seek your barometer. The most pain I have ever experienced is tied between a bone marrow test and watching my daughter skate at Nationals with a 102 fever, no concept of up or down, and getting two deductions for lifts that were too long, because she couldn't let go of her partner.

A five for me right now might be coming home after volunteering at the Alternative Education Center and sitting through two episodes of "Corner Gas" to spend time with my husband. This is probably tied in the pain meter to opening the closet door and seeing my daughter's gold waltz dress that cost $2,800.00, plus the cost of three trips to New York for design and fittings for an additional $1,000.00. I'm not going to add those figures together; I told my ninth-grade Algebra teacher that I would only do math once a day in my regular life as the world is about words and not numbers. Besides, I get sharp stabs that go through my chest as I ponder, will she wear this again on the ice or will her future husband understand the necessity of buying flowers that match Vienna gold?

My son just had his wisdom teeth out and this again gave me a pain factor of four. Oh, not from watching him suffer. He really didn't know what happened since he was asleep, but from fetching and running and answering his questions: No, sleeping on your right side will not give you a dry socket. No, having two pillows instead of three will not give you a dry socket. Yes, you can eat solid food on your fifth day, and you no longer have to chew like a rabbit using only your front teeth. My son, who at 19 has only been sick once in his life, would probably say his wisdom teeth extraction rates a seven on the pain scale. Of course, he also told me his legs hurt more than his jaw, because he went snowboarding the day before, and no, oddly enough, having pain somewhere else in your body will not induce the onset of dry sockets.

So, I really think asking a potential heart attack victim to rate the level of pain on the ten scale is without merit unless some background work is established.

I told the nurse giving the EKG that I was a "four," and she seemed unimpressed. I tired to explain that it is difficult to compare tangible with intangibles and that seeing the gold dress hanging on a wooden hanger in a dollar store dust bag is really hard to surpass.

She seemed to comprehend. Perhaps, I thought initially, she had a daughter who skated. But then she called for a wheelchair, and I heard her tell the attendant that I might be hallucinating.

"Oh come on, this is much worse than thinking you are getting a dry socket from sleeping on a 200-count pillowcase. This is much worse than finding 40 crystals on the dressing room floor the first the first time a dress is worn or seeing another 20 on the ice and not being able to get to them."

I was wheeled away and given some apple juice and three baby aspirin to chew. After evaluating the situation for a few more minutes, I told the ER nurse that I was wrong, my pain level was really only a three.

My anxiety level had lessened when I realized I did, in fact, have on clean underwear, which I knew would satisfy my own mother.

Ugly Elves

Nothing defines "family" as much as putting up the December holiday decorations. To be sure, we have boxes of ornaments from "all things Christmas past."

We probably have 8,000 skating ornaments, none purchased by said skater in the family; in fact, none even sanctioned by said skater as being needed or wanted.

We have the usual array of canine motif holiday bones with names of dogs now in the great play park in the sky, unleashed and unfettered.

We have the macaroni bells with green and red yarn, a Christmas macaroni "lei" suitable for a Kraft dinner at home, constructed by the kids in first or second grade. We have the stucco handprints crafted in art class in the third grade, and the orange juice can lids decorated by hammer and nail in the fourth grade.

These are not the problem. Glitter skates, painted noodles, and tin-punched stars all tactfully fill out the holes in our tree, especially on the backside facing the wall. The problem is the little pieces of holiday spirit that my husband has collected through the years.

Some men add football, baseball, or NASCAR memorabilia to the Christmas tree, a cute little NFL jersey, a blue car with a painted number. A simple touch. One that brings a smile when observed by a visitor.

My husband is a bit different.

My husband collects ugly Christmas ornaments like those older women who horde cats until the health department finally comes and removes 4,000 felines from the house and the only reason they give is just, "I couldn't turn any away; they were purring."

His favorite items are those old wax figures that originally looked a bit like soldiers, snow men, and Santa Claus. Over time the features melt a bit and fade until they resemble something that most kids suspect hide in their closets or under their beds in the middle of the night.

My husband insists on hanging them on the front of the tree.

When he sees my left eye twitching, he pre-empts my questions.

"They're vintage; you can't even buy these anymore. They're quite a collector's item."

I hesitate for a moment because, after all, he has lived through some of my alleged "collections" that turned out to be merely a Ty stuffed animal invasion. (Now the only thing they are good for is tossing on the ice after a competition.)

Still, this is not the time to be judicious.

"They look like melted marshmallow blobs. Can't we hang them in the back next to the purple skates and decoupaged milkbones?"

This is where it always gets weird.

"Stop it," my husband whispers and moves closer to the tree, as if I'm either going to grab them and throw them in the fireplace, or he wants to cover their little elf ears because I might be hurting their feelings.

My husband loves them all, from their muted little waxy distortions, to their twisted and decomposing styro-foamed balled bodies.

"They need to be out for Christmas to spread joy," he continues as he straightens a forty-year old piece of plastic holly on a reindeer's cock-eyed head.

"It will be bad luck if they aren't."

I am then rendered mute. What can I say? I am pretty sure this could be a script for a Hallmark movie. Man rescues unloved and discarded Christmas ornaments from the trash of those who have moved on to newer and brighter ornaments: ones that move, ones that are "limited edition." Ones that can withstand the temperatures of attic storage eleven months out of the year. Man is blessed throughout the year, while those who scoff get flat tires, chain letters, and a year of bed-head hair.

Three years ago, a plastic Snowman was glued to the ribbon that came with a box of holiday chocolates one of my students gave to me, hoping no doubt to move his grade from a 58 percent to one which hinted that he might graduate. Since the box looked untampered with, I ripped off the ribbon and tossed it in the trash.

My husband rescued the poly figure hours later after only a splash of marinara sauce had stained the body. I silently cursed myself for craving the peanut chews and not covering the figure with more garbage.

"What happened?" He queried all of us soulfully.

The three of us looked at each while trying to devise a silent group lie.

We looked at the translucent snowman that, if purchased at the dollar store, would have been packaged in lots of a thousand.

I sighed and took one for the team.

"Oh, I wondered where he went, he must have got tangled in the ribbon."

"He is very, very light, almost like a snowflake."

My son started to shake with laughter. My daughter started to back out of the circle thinking there are positive factors to adoption that have not all been explored. I gave them both the English Teacher glare until they folded, like a butterfly back into the group.

My husband smoothed the red sauce over the round stomach and rubbed it almost clean. "We're going to have to be very careful with this one," he said as he sat it gingerly on the shelf with the folk village. If it were in true scale, it would be as if Godzilla had come to town in the form of mountainous snow balls.

This year, as we unpack the boxes of ornaments, I am the first to unwrap the saved snowman. His stomach now bears a faint shadow of red, as if he may have enjoyed a big piece of cherry pie before braving the cold again in the holiday train village.

I hold him to the light and notice he, too, is losing some of his definition, a sign of the ages I guess. I take him to the village garden and place his smiling face with the strolling minstrels and pond skaters. He towers over them with an affable grin.

As I said, nothing defines "family" like putting up holiday decorations.

Enjoy the memories.

Opposites Attract

We have entered the world of "professional informality."
I'm not sure what this really means, but I am surmising the first step was Casual Friday, where employees started wearing denim and flat-soled shoes. This has currently mutated, of course, into flip-flops and tube tops for some establishments, mostly eating establishments that serve beer in long-necked bottles.

As a "professional" I maintain an email with the rather mundane symbols of my name. For some reason, I am permitted to use the first three letters of my name and then my entire last name. The problem with this is I am reduced to "She," which you have to admit is a bit Tarzan and Jane. I am the female Bosley, not to be mistaken for the "He" Bosley. I often receive emails from people with the web monikers of LetzbringSeXybck and 2hot2not, and I struggle with the return salutation. This forces me to open my cyber responses with witty verbiage like, "Hey there" which descends into another level of "casual."

Professional informality then becomes another example of the oxymorons that invade our lives.

I am the queen of the oxymoron.

My kingdom of proof: I drive a convertible Volvo, the safest sedan made until you add the rag-top. I am perpetually on a diet, but continue to gain weight. I teach Journalism at my school, but we don't put out a newspaper. I also teach English, yet my students won't read. My garden has tomatoes that won't turn red, and I have a pool, but I cannot swim.

Trust me, there is a story in each of those.

We have been fed oxymorons all of our lives.

"You are pretty on the inside."

"This hurts me more than it hurts you."

"It's not you, it's me."

"It's nice to grow old gracefully."

Let's be honest, we've come to expect the lies and swallow them greedily like drive-thru French fries on the way home from Weight Watchers.

Still, it makes the whole dress code policy a shadowed document. We, for example, are not permitted to wear "flip-flops."

"Could you define that?" one of my co-workers asked our boss.

"Well," he pondered. "I think that means if it makes that sound when you walk, you know, the one that sounds like chewing gum and then popping it."

My friend and I exchanged glances. "So," she continued, "then it is really about the sound produced?"

"That's it!" our boss smiled, nodded, and sauntered into his office.

So, adding to my list of oxymorons, I wear flips that do not flop.

Logic

"Logic" is a funny word that we often banter about.

The unusual thing about logic is that we use it as a noun and as a verb in a manner of speaking. You can "use logic" or "it can be logical."

Oddly enough, I have been caught up in the concept that we usually do not apply logic when we use these terms.

And, of course, to add to the subplot, men and women sometimes see logic differently.

Three weeks ago, while I was at the grocery store, my husband had a heart attack. On the way home, I met an ambulance on our two-lane country road, and I had a premonition that it was somehow connected to my house — narcissism at its worst. I berated myself for the remainder of the two-mile journey for this voice of doom in my ear.

It wasn't logical at all.

Even after I arrived home, there were no real neon arrows of alarm. There were no crowds of neighbors on the corner, no notes taped to the door that said, "While you were out." Actually, everything seemed pretty much in order except that my husband wasn't anywhere to be found. This was a bit of an annoyance on my third trip into the house with the case of water, carton of kitty litter, and litany of perishables thrown in those 1/12 ply blue shopping bags that lose their poly bond once they leave the air quality of the chain store.

My daughter, home for the day from skating all week and trained from the world of CSI being set in seemingly every city in the United States, checked the last number dialed on our portable house phone and discovered it was 9-1-1.

It is not logical to believe that time stood still, but it did.

At least, that is, until I answered the phone that started ringing seconds after our discovery. A dispatcher from the emergency medical center told me that husband was being transported to one of two hospitals in our county.

It is not logical to forget to turn onto a road you have driven fifty times a week for the past twenty years, nor is it logical to make deals with whomever is willing to make them in your call to muses.

I arrived at the hospital to be told my husband was being medivaced to the heart trauma center in Baltimore. The doctors felt he had a blockage and advised he would be out of surgery before I could drive the forty-five mile distance.

The nurses handed me a plastic bag that contained some of his clothes and advised me that they were sorry, but they had to cut off his sweatshirt. When I had left that morning, my husband had been working in the yard, wearing his jeans with the knees ripped out, (not Alan Jackson mode) and his zip-up Old Navy sweatshirt that had been bleached, ripped, stretched out, hit by the weed-eater, repeatedly buried under the bags of weekly trash (by me) and rescued and salvaged triumphantly (by him). His gravitation to bagman couture while gardening is not logical since he has at least twenty shirts and sweatshirts with tags hanging in the closet.

"I'm saving them," he would say.

"Why don't you just throw out your yard-wear and start wearing some of your older shirts as yard clothes. Your new clothes with the price tags still on them are now five or six years old."

He would just look at me. "That doesn't make any sense to use perfectly good clothes for yard work (synonym for "that is not logical").

I looked at the nurse.

"You had to throw it away?"

She nodded, not telling me what I suspected, that the medical staff had not thought the biohazard bags could contain it.

Still, it was not logical to feel teary-eyed over a misshapen rag that had escaped the trash bin by some seemingly magic power akin to having nine lives. But, at that moment, I likened it to Superman's cape.

I do not remember the drive to Charm City. I am assuming I did all the correct things. I can only surmise that somewhere there is a logical portion of our brains that takes over and guides the other part, the paralyzed part, to go on.

The doctors were right. By the time I arrived at the second hospital, my husband had two stents put in a major artery and was on the mend. When I walked into the ICU he was actually awake and worried that the tractor and his garden tools were still scattered on the lawn.

Yes, three weeks ago the world stood on its edge for a period of time. It does not seem logical that my husband could go back to work on Monday, but trust me, he really needed to go.

We have much to be thankful for. Now, twenty-one days later, I am tempted to send a thank you card to the nurses for cutting up that awful sweatshirt.

He, on the other hand, ponders how medical science has developed a procedure that can move surgical devices through a minute vein from a small incision in the leg yet cannot fathom how to use the zipper on a shirt that clearly had many years of life left in it.

"It's just not logical," he says.

That so true, I think.

Park It

Hospitals display some unusual factors these days.

For one thing, they have the smallest number of handicapped parking spaces. You might argue that they don't need them, since most people are driven by relatives for admissions or transported by an ambulance, but in a society that seems programmed to issue handicapped parking decals and plates to what seems like 60 percent of the population, I beg to differ.

Our town has a small, one-story mall with a proportionally sized parking lot. Every morning "mall walkers" arrive in mass and fill all the handicapped parking spots in their pursuit of their daily cardio work-out of three to five miles of closed-shop sprinting.

The irony, or course, is these velour workout-suit clad walkers get angry if all the handicapped spaces are occupied, because it means they will have to, well, walk a longer distance, perhaps 20 feet or more, to the mall entrance door so they can begin their walking route.

So, I was a bit shocked to see only five handicapped parking spaces in the visitor parking lot at a large metropolitan hospital. Our local Starbucks have three handicapped spots right in front of the stores, which seems to be a three-to-fifteen ratio compared to a five-to-five hundred ratio for the hospital. I haven't really processed the symbolism of this yet, but it seems to center on the degree of the ailment, and hospitals aren't going to fool around with those who get a hang-tag for something as minor as an ingrown toenail anymore than a church usher is going to make change from the offering plate.

Another unusual factor about hospitals today is they are not like the ones depicted on television. No "Grey's Anatomy," "ER," or "Private Practice" lobbies. The patient rooms are not like the Ritz-Carlton, which would allow you to build, say, a large dollhouse like on a recent episode of one such drama. There are very few single rooms, and the doubles will not accommodate a family of eight, like a recent showing of "Greys' Anatomy," where George's family congregate with the pack of seven doctors.

I have not been a patient for several years, so I was stunned to learn that hospitals now have room service. Seriously. Years ago you were given a daily menu card and small dull golf pencil. An orderly wearing what looked like a shower cap would come around and collect them by bed number. If you forgot to check off an item, like salt or pepper, cream for your coffee, or mayonnaise, it was just too bad. Today, you can call down to the kitchen, place an order, and they will bring up whatever you want with all the condiments, just like you are staying at the Hilton. Unlike the Hilton, you don't have to set the empty tray in the hallway and worry about tripping over it in the morning.

Another amazing feature of hospitals du jour is the spa treatment. Well, this means you get back rubs. But twenty minute backrubs, not the puny two minute kneadings you get if you ask your spouse to rub your neck.

And you get lotion with the massage.

True, the staff still wears latex gloves, but after a few minutes I can imagine you would forget the sterile coolness and get lost in the mere joy of having your muscles soothed from spending several hours of strenuous resting in a craftmatic type of bed and watching free cable TV.

So, it seems plausible that with the rising cost of airfare, hotel rooms, and rental cars, that folks could just stay close to home for a little vacation. That's right. You could decide to have a bit of elective surgery done if no real ailment presents itself and wallow in the lap of luxury for a few days, enjoying a bed that can transform into 83 positions, ordering room service, watching TV at your set volume, and getting daily massages.

The only problem would be if you have handicapped relatives that need visitor parking.

Izzy Bits Bosley

Barking Up The Wrong Tree

Back in the winter, I was in a bit of the doldrums and decided to get another dog. This proved to be one of the most momentous decisions of my life.

Some people, I am told, have affairs during mid-life reckonings, some get powerful sports cars when they previously owned a Buick LaSabre, and some get implants in various or all places.

I, in some odd twist on the concept, got a dog.

I am a dog person by design and choice. This is easy to confirm because most of my coffee mugs have one dog or another painted on them, I own and actually wear dresses with dog motifs on them, and I have several thousand dollars of dog art accosting my walls. (Most of this was before skating took over of course.) I am an AKC licensed dog judge, and people come to me with "dog" questions. The problem is that we have always had good dogs, translated to mean calm dogs. We have had working breeds in the form of Great Danes or Dobermans or, as now, a non-sporting dog, a white Standard Poodle.

Working breeds are typically like non-sporting dogs, in that the essence of their day is deciding where they will snooze next: the bed, the new chair, or the couch cushion.

With my daughter going away to college, which really means she will never come home because she is really ice skating more than she is colleging, and my son graduating from high school and the potential of the freshman 15 has found its way to my thighs times two, I decided I needed a little pick-me-up.

A little puppy-pick-me-up. You know, the smell of puppy feet and puppy breath. The little pink tongue, unconditional love, never packing to go to a university or an ice-rink.

I know. I could have gone with that sexy convertible. I could have gone with a spa membership or some Pilates and yoga lessons.

I went with the Fox Terrier.

This is not a breed that I am really familiar with. In fact, you don't see many of them in the real world. You do see their calmer cousins, the Jack Russells (now officially called the Parson's Terrier). After years of losing our gentle giant Great Dane companions at seven and eight years old, my bruised heart ached for something with longevity.

I made some calls in my dog network and was told the same thing.

"Are you crazy? You don't want to get one of those."

This, of course, made it more appealing. I needed the distraction. I wanted to be pulled out of my empty-nest-dreading stupor into the demanding task of Frisbee throwing and flydog.

I was guided to a breeder in California who had two litters at the time. She emailed me photos, and I was captivated by the liquid brown eyes of the canine infants.

"Wire nine hundred dollars and I'll ship your little girl this weekend."

Wire money? Since I don't have any secret bank accounts in the Cayman Islands, this was a new procedure for me. In the past, I have dealt with credit cards, checks, and money orders. This is the modern age, I told myself, get with it.

During the week, pre money wiring, I talked with the

breeder everyday or through email. She offered assurances of all kinds of networking and support once the puppy arrived for the litany of new adventures that awaited: ear-gluing, table stacking (for shows), and hand-stripping as a grooming skill.

Once the puppy arrived, and we confirmed she was safe and healthy, we have never heard from the breeder and entourage again.

And I almost understand why.

Had she called the first month, I would probably have told her it wasn't working out. I did, in fact, need at least four hours sleep every night and ten fingers, although I feared the loss of two that were constantly falling into the terrier's mouth when she jumped waist high in her constant battle with trying to keep four feet off the ground. I would have told her it was unsettling to have a ten-pound dog launch itself at you from shadowed corners or the stairs, often getting tangled in your hair like those bats that originate in Transylvania. I would have told her that it is not humane to deliver an animal to people that does not EVER sleep, an animal in fact, that seems allergic to sleep.

Of course now, the wired money makes perfect sense. If I had charged the purchase I could probably have convinced a Visa customer service representative that I had been mislead, had an act of fraud committed against my person. This was not a dog delivered by American Airlines, but a sonic set of teeth attached to fur.

In desperation, I did make one attempt to contact the breeder. After several misadventures trying to leash break my Terror-ier I found it was a task I could not do. Attaching a cord to her collar was like lighting a gasoline soaked rag and trying to hang on to it.

"I just wanted to ask if there is some special leash you use to train the puppies ..." I sighed into the answering machine droning on the other end. Like maybe Wonder Woman's magic lasso I thought.

No response. No reply. I suspect the breeder has now retired and is living in Hawaii with a team of miniature poodles and a cadre of wired money from frantic people all over the United States.

My daughter, home for the day a week ago, remarked, "Mom there's weird white hair on the back of the couch, how does she get up there?"

I sighed and looked up at the ceiling fan remembering what I had found there the day before. But since this is my folly, I can't admit just how far it has gone.

"I don't think they're Izzy's hair, Babes, I think; they're probably mine."

Bright Lights

Pilar and I just returned from our annual pilgrimage to New York City.

The part of me that wishes that I had nurtured the love of architecture and the knowledge of the 12 kinds of vegetable squash in my children would love to say we wandered the streets noting the granite cornices and unique columns of century old buildings. I would love to proffer that we ferried out and saluted our most grand gift from France, the noble lady of the harbor, Miss Liberty.

But alas, we did not.

Instead, we journeyed, as in Oz, to visit the wizard.

The wizard in this case is the fabulous Tania Bass, creator of extraordinary costumes of dancers, skaters, and actresses around the world.

Let me clarify a bit here; we have had exquisite costumes designed and crafted in the past by masters in the field. Our crystal count last year alone had me x-rayed, scanned, puffed, and sniffed at every domestic airport through which we traveled. But the yellow-bricked costume road had never led us to doors as golden as those of Ms. Bass.

At the beginning of the new skating season, my daughter asked if she could have one dress made by the New York magician. I probably paled a bit, but with new highlights in my hair, it probably wasn't that noticeable. One size 1 dress, I thought. How expensive can that be?

"I want her to create my waltz dress. She will make something special," my daughter explained.

"A waltz dress," I pondered. Good choice, I decided. If she had asked for a Free Dance costume, it would be dated to a Rock theme, or an OD costume would be limited to some traditional folk ballad, and therefore get limited wear. A waltz dress is universal and can be worn for several years, perhaps even when she gets married. A waltz dress is all about flow and has a certain cut to the back, all the elements of a wedding gown I consoled myself.

"That's a good idea. Maybe you should get white this year."

"Mom, coaches don't like white on the ice, it gets lost sometimes with all that white on white. They want me to get something that pops so that when I step on the ice, the judges get an initial impression of exquisiteness."

"Really, that sounds like an expensive feature; maybe we could just add more beads."

We took the train to the city from Philadelphia and walked to Tania's 36th street design studio, tugging Samsonite and Vera Bradley duffle bags.

If I only had the words to describe the salon. It is the Willy Wonka Chocolate World transformed to fashion wonderland. There are millions of beckoning crystals, a thousand bolts of tantalizing fabrics, miles of embellished trim, and costumes and photographs adorning every wall.

It is a magical place where magical things are promised to happen.

Tania Bass looked at my daughter and asked what color she was thinking of (I had stopped thinking about green, the color of the cash in my wallet, and moved on to blue, the color of my checks that I was going to write to add to the cash in my wallet).

My daughter looked in Tania's eyes and replied. "I was thinking gold this year, a beautiful rich gold, not a yellow or brass color."

Tania smiled at my daughter as if she had answered the secret riddle and then went behind the counter and from some hidden recess produced a bolt of fabric the color of an iridescent sun as it sets on a gulf coast. She then draped an inch wide piece of trim across the front of the fabric and talked beading patterns that shifted in the arena lights.

After the measurements, Tania sat on a small stool in front of us and took out an unadorned book. In five minutes she had sketched a dress so exquisite even Leonardo Di Vinci would have marveled at its proportional perfection.

Like witnessing any wonder of the world, I was dazed, and did not mind writing a deposit check that was slightly more than my monthly mortgage payment. We may have actually skipped to the hotel on 45th street because people did move over as if they were encountered munchkins on the yellow brick road.

The remainder of the trip was a bit anticlimactic after meeting the wizard. We did go to a comedy club and were part of the show in our front row seats. We did see "Wicked" (irony at its best), but my daughter was more impressed that Eva Longoria and Tony Parker were sitting in front of us.

"They're getting married in two weeks! Can you believe they are out on a date like regular people?

"Umh." I murmured absently thinking checking balances and savings accounts.

"Don't you just love her white dress? It is so simple, but stunning on her. I think people always look best when they stick to classic, simple lines, don't you?"

I sat for a moment thinking there were flying monkeys in the intermission scene as well, but I merely took a deep breath and answered her as best I could as my eye started to twitch.

"You're probably right, sweetie. Do you think they'll let me bring a drink from the bar back to my seat. I just need something basic?"

Sherry Bosley | 73

Pilar Bosley and John Corona rocking out on the ice

Temperatures Rising

If my husband and I ever get a divorce, it will not be because of affairs, gambling, or incessant snoring. It will be because I am too hot.

Oh, not in the Paris Hilton iconic catch-phrase type of hot. 'Hot' as in my Ban Solid deodorant is failing, I have sweat running down the middle of back, and I am considering cutting my clothes off with scissors type of hot.

It is just barely approaching summer and the debacle of thermostat control has reared its ugly head again.

In the winter, my husband wants the climate set at a "comfortable" 68 degrees. I have found that it is easier to brush your teeth in water that has not started to crystallize, but I gave up this argument years ago. I now wear layers of clothing, have flannel sheets, and eat soup with mittens on once we pass the winter solstice. I have even considered putting heated bricks under the covers like Jane Eyre, but gave up on this idea once I discovered the fireplace is merely for "show" and actually sucks the heat from the rest of the house rendering the temperature 60 degrees in the uppermost corner bedroom.

The oddity of the situation is that in the summer we should then be able to reside in the same pleasant temperature we established in the winter: 68 degrees. Not so. In a twist of conventional logic, the "correct" temperature for summer habitation (per my life partner) is 74 degrees.

This is not comfortable. My husband says that my inner-body thermostat has become maladjusted because I have sat in ice rinks for decades.

This is the temperature that makes those red Christmas candles you left out all year start to melt and sway left in the candelabra. This is the temperature that makes ants pack up and head to an abode that has free utilities included in the rent. This is a temperature that almost sends you to Macy's to buy a new bathing suit.

My husband swears his thermostat commandeering is founded in the principle of saving the environment. I suspect that it is grounded in the recent 50 percent electric rate hike.

Like any good wife I have offered helpful advice to assist in keeping our utility bills low. For example, he could skip watching golf tournaments every weekend on television, I mean really, every Sunday is the culmination of some Open, or Masters, or Classic, somewhere. He could actually wait until the ten o'clock news and find out the results and view the highlight reel. He could also forego his obsessions with "Family Guy" and "Scrubs" reruns. With a bit of modification, we could probably have the thermostat down to 73 degrees at no additional cost.

I readily admit that we have become a spoiled nation. We like our comforts. Most of us did not grow up with them. My family did not have central air-conditioning in the house; my parents had a small window unit in their bedroom that they used without guilt to the exclusion of the rest of us, who sat in sweat-pooled puddles on vinyl kitchen clad chairs before the open ice-box door. (This would not happen today. Today parents would install units in children's bedrooms to the exclusion of themselves, and they would take second jobs to get them oscillating air flow.) Our cars also did not have air-conditioning. My sister and I craved trips in the backseat of the Corvair, risking dragonflies, bees, and discarded cigarette butts, just for that feeling of moving current. As a parent I often start the car five minutes before our departure so the vehicle will be at the right temperature when my kids enter.

It is true, we all get spoiled for our creature comforts and once we have them, we don't want to give them back or give them up.

I proffer to you that if blood could boil it would probably be at about 100 degrees centigrade.

But I suspect it starts to roll a bit at 74 degrees Fahrenheit.

Life and marriage is about compromise and restructuring goals.

I have turned a blind eye to the luxury lawn tractor that sits in our shed that has halogen headlights (although I don't recall any midnight grass snipping ever occurring on our lawn), cup holders, and a lumbar comfort seat. I have remained mum when my husband bought new golf irons that allegedly added ten yards to his fairway drives, and I have been mute about the fact that greens fees are often 20 times the price of a movie admission.

I have compromised by living the life of a lumberjack in the winter, and now that the heat index is approaching triple digits, I would like to feel as if I could sit and have a mint julep, so to speak, without the ice melting faster than the glaciers north of Greenland.

I am petitioning for 72 degrees and control of the thermostat during the summer months. Perhaps on my birthday in August, I could even have a day at 70 degrees. I like to live right of the cusp of needing a sweater.

Anyway, those are my demands that I will give to the mediator.

Sometimes being "hot" is not all that cool.

Princess and the P

As I sit here, I see cobwebs hanging from my ceiling.
Well, just a few in the corners. In another place and time I would have immediately retrieved my dust wand and swept them from their moors. But I am older and wiser now. I know it is a futile mission. Plus, the Martha Stewart side of me realizes that it will be Halloween in another month, and you can't buy decorations like that.

No, so many things keep getting pushed back in the order of priority. I used to take *everything* off the shelves to dust *every* square inch of mahogany surface. Now, I make a quick pass or get a lower watt light bulb. I used to arrange my drawers and prioritize my closet by seasons, now I use the basic hunt and peck system or take whatever is on top. My own mother would be horrified to know that often my undergarments do not match in color.

She would also be scandalized to know we stopped the Sunday night dinner long ago. This, of long tradition in my family lineage, to consist of the red meat of the day, in large quantities, a green vegetable, usually a bit on the mushy side, bread and butter, mashed potatoes (really mashed not whipped), some type of corn dish, gravy made from "pan drippings," and dessert.

The dessert was the first to go. By this, I don't mean eliminated it; I mean substituted with a bakery section selection.

Then the red meat changed to chicken sans gravy.

The green became a salad as the bread became croutons.

And the potato became rice.

These are our basic meal choices:

Baked or grilled chicken. Marinated or plain.

Green salad with Ranch or Italian dressing.

We have lost all spontaneity of eating.

We have lost all purpose in cleaning.

It is all such a repetitive cycle, one that seems to go on forever without appreciation or assistance.

You may sense I'm falling into the doldrums a bit.

My daughter came home for the weekend, and it was a bit like the princess and the pea.

I had spent an inordinate amount of time of making the house look warm and welcoming. I had a *huge* vase of roses sitting on the dining table, an autumn cornucopia on the game table in the great room, and fresh baked scones. Okay, I made up the last item, but I would have if Safeway didn't already make the best muffins in the world.

The house smelled of Lemon Pledge and scented candles. This is a necessity in our house, because we have a geriatric dog that, if human, would talk incessantly about her weak bladder and periodontal problems.

My daughter immediately asked what "that smell" was.

"What smell?" I asked leaning toward my new cinnamon candle like Vanna White reaching for a vowel.

"I don't know," she said. "It smells like Chinese food or old people."

I blew out the candle in case it had been mislabeled.

When she was going to bed later she called out to me from her room.

"Mom, there is cat hair all over my bed."

"Well, they like to sleep in there when you aren't home," I offered. "I guess it is their way to stay close to you."

"Yuck", she said as she tossed a pillow and a teddy bear on the floor giving me a look that Mrs. Brady never passed on to Alice. "It's disgusting".

A few minutes later she called out again.

"Mom, where did you get this pillow?"

"Well, it was one of the guest pillows in the closet. You took yours, remember."

"Geez, it's really hard. And it has cat hair on it."

"Really," I answered. "I guess the cats don't mind it then."

I could feel her eyes on me through the wall. "I'll make sure I vacuum your bed each week from now on."

"Thanks," she said.

And there you have it: the daughter of an English teacher missed the lesson on satire.

Recycle

I have encountered a paradoxical situation.

I cannot throw away my trash can.

Our trash cans are on the "outside" so they fall under the care of my husband in our version of Robert's Rules of Household Tasks. Don't get me wrong, my husband is a perfectionist at cleaning, weeding, and mowing.

People have even sworn they have witnessed him dusting behind the shutters on the third floor. When he mows or vacuums, he creates those patterns you see at ballparks. When he was ten, he actually asked his mother for a set of velvet ropes so he could clean his room and "rope" it off from traffic.

Saying he is fastidious is low-balling it.

So, it is hard to explain how the equipment at our house looks like third world rejects. He has a rake with three prongs. The shovel is now worn down to half its former scoop. He has tied the grass shield up a few inches on the riding lawn mover with some bright orange left-over cable wire.

We bought our trash cans the year we were married. In fact, I think I have blotted from my schema the fact that he probably bought them for me as a wedding present. These are not the shiny silver cans that look like beacons in the moonlight. These are the large gray/brown plastic receptacles that look like they could double as hippo huts. The plastic has actually worn away in areas, whether from acid rain, or just giving in to the litany of items we toss in our trash vats.

I'm not sure how long we have been without a wheel or two. I have grown accustomed to wheeling them up the driveway like a clown of a unicycle. We have lost one lid in a March wind, and all of the handles. There is a huge crack down the side of one that resulted in a snag-and-grab of my silk blouse last April.

That, of course, was the last straw. That is when I decided to can the cans.

My husband behaved like a French national at a Bush speech.

"There is nothing wrong with the cans. They hold trash. They don't need to look pretty."

"This isn't about looks. This is about practicality. We have no lid, we have no wheels. We are digging furrows in the ground every week when we put them out. This is ridiculous."

In protest, I decided to get rid of the trash cans.

This has become the bane of my existence.

Leaving them out for several days did not result in a theft. In fact, a neighbor put them back in our driveway, presumably in a good Samaritan Act to keep the community beautiful.

I tried to fit them in my car to take somewhere — maybe Goodwill — but they won't fit.

In frustration, I left a post it note on one of them saying "Take These" on trash day.

When I came home they were sitting empty at curb, listing badly like two wrecked cars at the defunct junk yard.

The next week, I taped a white 8 1/2 by 11 piece of paper with the words "TRASH THESE CANS" in black Sharpie.

When I came home, one of the cans was tossed about 20 feet up into our yard and the second one was partially jammed against our mailbox. This one had a hole knocked in the side.

My neighbor later told me that the trash men were playing "bull fighter" using my cans as the cape and the truck as the brawny bull.

For my last attempt, I took my Sharpie and wrote on each

can, "These are trash, please take."

When I came home, the trash cans were sitting like rusted out 73 Olds Cutlasses, blocking the driveway.

There was a note taped to my mailbox.

"We'll bring a recycling schedule for you next week. Tuesdays are for trash only."

When the world gives you lemons ...

Trump Card

So when you have two children – one who skates, and one who doesn't – the one without the blades is basically in the power seat.

That's right. Because he is aware that his sister is basically getting the equivalent of a 700 series BMW each year. Okay, maybe a high end 500 series.

Still, he knows you aren't going to quibble about a $700 snowboard, a new laptop, or concert tickets.

No. He keeps that trump card in his pocket and plays it at just the right time. And that trump card is how few his demands really are. He plays high school sports. It is hard for skating parents to believe this, but the school loans you the uniform and everyone looks alike. The most it costs for a season of play is $100.00, and most of that is for fundraising candy, pizza kits, or candles.

Non-skating children hate to watch skating competitions.

They dislike it on DVDs, on television, or in person. They hate listening to conversations about free dances, costumes, and other teams. They typically leave the room and probably go online to some website called mysiblingskatesandthatisour-life.com. But of course, before they leave the room they give you that look, you know, like you are an ice addict and need help.

My own son has found several ways to torture me. What

he fails to understand is that I loved skating before I even had children. The fact that the two intersected seems almost accidental. There are some sports I do not like, or at least, that I do not like to watch. He has found ways to join almost all of them.

In the winter, when it is typically 20 degrees outside, he is on the high school swim team. His school doesn't have a pool, so he is bused to practice at another facility. All of his meets are at one of two facilities, both thirty minutes away. (He has pointed out that this is half the distance of the rink where his sister skated.)

I'm not sure how many of you have been to an indoor swimming pool in the middle of winter when they are having a swim meet. For me, it goes something like this:

I arrive in a winter coat because it is freezing outside and there is typically a mile walk from the parking lot. I enter the building and the humidity completely evaporates any Lady Speed Stick that I had left under my arms.

I find the last available space on the overhead bleachers that are suspended 40 feet above the pool. I remove my coat and then find out that four more people have decided to cram in on the same bench. If my bra strap slips down I must ask the woman sitting behind me to pull it up.

There is this annoying buzzer that announces the start of each race, and each race typically takes about one minute. It's impossible to know when your child is swimming, because they all wear the same suit, cap, and goggles, and when they are in the water, all you see are eight swim caps. Typically, 8,000 kids swim at each meet.

After about 10 minutes, my asthma kicks in, and I start wheezing. Oh yes, I do have skating induced asthma as well. You do not have to step on the ice to fall victim to the stresses of skating.

I typically make it twenty minutes before I have to get up, losing my place on the bench forever, as the crowd regroups like a scoop out of Marshmallow Fluff. I stumble to the door with labored breathing, as if I have just finished the 500 medley instead of some boy in a white cap who I hope was my son.

It is only after five minutes of steam coming from my body that I realize I have left my coat inside and must return, paying another four dollars, to retrieve my coat.

In the fall, my son is on the cross country team. This means they run in all weather and on all terrains, except anything hard surfaced, or safe, or clean.

Today, it was raining.

Today they had a meet. A fifteen-school meet.

I had to park two miles away to watch the meet.

"Watching" is the trick phrase here.

It was like the scene from "Braveheart," where they all run down the hill. I had my camera ready as literally 150 boys ran straight down the hill to follow some little trail that disappeared in the woods after 20 feet. They ran four or five miles supposedly. And that was it.

I watched a mob scene, and then they disappeared in the outback country to emerge again 20 minutes later.

Did I mention it was raining?

When the boys reemerged, they were mud splattered and soaked.

I was mud splattered and soaked.

Plus I was out of breath from walking from the car, and I was dreading the walk back. I was also slightly missing the swim meet when I was almost dry.

So there is my punishment. My son has picked sports that are unwatchable. Even when I go, I can't see him, or if I do, I don't know it.

No one calls his name over the public address system. No one claps or cheers.

I am now worried about spring. I found a flyer on his desk for spelunking.

Maybe I'll just buy him a BMW and we'll call it even.

Pilar Bosley putting the finishing touches on Clare Farrell's make-up for the Lake Placid competition

Color Forms

Okay, so I was wrong.

There is something else that is expensive in skating.

We will put this in the broad category of "Cosmetics." This includes make-up, skin care products, hair products (including appliances), hair cuts, and hair color. Oh, I forgot to mention "tanning," as an action verb which should mean lying on the beach in Cabo St. Lucus but actually means a tanning bed or (sigh) a blast from bronzing sprayer.

Yes, we forget to put these items in the household budget.

I know you all have stories here.

The problem for ice dancers is that we must add these expenses on top of skating bills.

Skaters have to look tan because the ice makes them look "washed out." They can't look too tan or judges might think they are "frivolous" and don't spend enough time on the ice, or how could they get such a great tan.

Girls have to have a hairstyle that can easily adapt to the classic ballerina bun for some compulsory dances, yet be ready to be spit-curled with a Spanish flair for a tango, Paso, or samba beat. The Free-dance and OD must look carefree, yet not get in the way of the eyes, mouth, and face.

It is a paradox.

The color must be right also. Partners must look alike as if they were one unit working like Siamese twins.

Partners must look different to show the strengths of each person making one united team, hence the red hair phase for one partner.

Partners aren't sure, so put in some highlights so it looks like they did something.

And then, there are the appliances and enhancements. A Chi hair straightener is $140.00 (and, by the way, it does not plug in, even with an adapter, in Europe). Travel hot rollers are a bargain at $40.00. But, then you have the crystal hair clips and bows, which, as we all know can be anywhere from $20 to $200 a piece.

Yes, I know. I have a bath clip I bought at Walgreens fifteen years ago for $2.99. It is brown plastic and looks a bit trailer trash next to some of these Austrian sparklers, but it does the job and keeps my hair from hitting the water.

The skin care line is the actual backbone of any make-up regimen, but of course, these kids have no wrinkles or lines. They exercise, so their skin is well oxygenated and hydrated. The only thing unhealthy is actually wearing skating competition make-up for too long and then they may get two clogged pores.

Even though they buy good make-up.

Really good. Mac and Smashbox. Bobbi Brown and Lancome.

With each costume comes the need for a whole line of eye and lip colors. When I was a girl, Cover Girl was the pushed by Cheryl Tiegs and nothing cost more than $3.99. You could look like a model if you bought it. Cover Girl Clean!

Now we have to add $500.00 for make-up, $500.00 for seasonal hair (Yes, it does change and grow from sectionals to nationals!) and another bill or two for the tan.

We now have to keep bangs trimmed, ends snipped, and hues highlighted to look "natural."

There are benefits though.

Sometimes they put free product samples in the bags and the girls pass them on to their moms.

Of course these are the products that are said to reduce winkles, stretch marks, and the signs of aging.

Ex-Wives

My husband was previously married.

This might shock some of my friends, because I have never even bought a used car. I do, however, trek to New York at least once a year and shop at some high end second-hand stores, where I have picked up a Chanel jacket, a St. John's suit, and this year, an in-demand bag.

Quality never goes out of style.

So, my husband has two children from his first marriage, and next Saturday his daughter is getting married. Now this is a joyous occasion. She is a sweet young woman and is marrying a wonderful man. They are both near 30 so they are not rushing into the moment.

There is a "but."

Next Saturday is also a *big* wedding anniversary for my husband and me. And although I had previously imagined the celebration in Fiji, renewing our vows, and him presenting me with an emerald and diamond eternity ring, I am certainly a big enough person to forget about that and "for the good of the children" celebrate at his ex-wife's house.

Oh, I forgot to mention that fact.

Yes. At the home of his ex-wife.

Well, home is not really the word. "Estate" is more descriptive. Yes, after her divorce, she upgraded and got the luxury model. Her second divorce settlement, twelve years ago, got the house, the cars, and enough money that she has never had to work again.

So the wedding is very formal, yet non-traditional. The bride is being "given-away" by her brother, and there are no other attendants. I believe the traditional father-daughter dance is now to be "Love Potion Number 9." The bride and groom are vegetarian, so we will later dine on tofu and feta cheese.

I say "believe" because we didn't get an invitation. The ex-wife said it "must have been lost in the mail." That is odd because the groom's best friend, albeit a bit wild, has a different post office and his was lost also.

This would all be bearable, except no other relatives from my husband's side of the family were invited. Although we sent an early contribution for the event, any additional assistance was declined.

Good times ahead.

So, I think you see the set-up here. I will be spending my anniversary in the back row at the ceremony and probably eating assorted grasses at the photographer's table.

Luckily, I won't have to be in any photos and wedding cake is my favorite of all cake species.

On the bright side of the eye of the storm, I think this warrants the Cartier Love bracelet I have been leaving hints for. After all, nothing symbolizes "eternity" like sitting in the home of an ex-spouse on your current anniversary.

Everything will be fine. Unless we wear the same dress.

Cropping Out

It looks like I am going to need to get a new camera before sectionals.

Remember my family reunion last weekend? Well, the photos are back, and there is a problem. A big one.

Typically, I am the one taking the photos. Looking through the old photo books, I am like the phantom. I establish the traditional shots in all the holiday pix. You know, the ones with the kids in red pajamas sipping cocoa by the yule fire, the first day of school, the birthday cake blow-outs — all captured.

In reverse, no one ever remembers the photographer. This has been a splendid arrangement.

Maybe when the kids are older, they will feel like a Disney cartoon character. Think about it, 90 percent of them didn't have a mother, but so far no one has noticed the omission.

Until last weekend.

Someone suggested a "group" shot. I volunteered to take the photo, but was instantly turned down because "Everyone has to be in the picture." This is made possible by the advancement of technology that allows a fifteen-second timer on cameras manufactured in the last eleven years. Well, that and a dry beach towel used to tilt the lens to the right angle.

I think that is where the problem came in. Maybe the beach towel wasn't really dry because when I got the photos back today there was a major distortion. Luckily, I guess, it was only over me. Apparently the water on the lens created this magnified effect that makes me look, well, larger than real life.

I know I can't really look that way because I can, of course, see myself in the mirror any time of the day. At no time has my reflection resembled that of a small harbor porpoise as it does in that picture. I mean if my hair were longer my relatives could tell strangers Kristie Alley came to their cook-out.

And it is a shame to ruin a good picture because of one little glitch.

Which is why I asked the photo clerk at Ritz to edit the 5x7 version with the same technique I heard they used on Katie Couric.

"What do you want me to do to it exactly?" the clerk asked.

"Well, I want you to make it look more like me. It's a bad angle or something."

I'm not sure he was feeling all that well, because he was sweating and a little flushed throughout the process, but eventually he came up with something that is a bit closer to my real weight, verified by my driver's license, which we all know is an official piece of identification.

My sister-in-law's arm looks a bit palsied now, but it is just slight blemish compared to original ballooned pose, and she won't mind.

So, I am going to have to buy another camera to prevent the possibility of any other distortions.

I mean, what if the camera blew my daughter up to a size 2?

I have to go to Best Buy to make the purchase, however. The photo clerk at the camera shop couldn't come up with an answer as to how this could happen in the first place. In fact, he didn't even try to guess, he just kept shaking his head.

Anyway, I think I'll go back to my role behind the camera. Sometimes I'll let a little bit of my pinky finger slide in for family shots.

The Kween

This is a sad day for me.

My idol of the skating world has basically all but announced her retirement. Michelle Kwan will skip the 2006-2007 competitive year. Everyone in skating knows what that really means. My daughter hyperventilates if she misses one day of practice, let alone a year. Taking a year off of skating, at 26 is basically taking your boots off in the competitive arena.

I am sad for a few reasons, as I suspect many of us are. I am sad that I bought tickets to last year's SkateAmerica to see her, and she withdrew the day the tickets arrived. I am sad I bought lower-box, all-event tickets for Nationals last year because, as we all know, she didn't skate. I have spent several hundred dollars to see Michelle not skate. And, I think we all wish she had been able to have that one last skate, when she knew, and we knew, that it would be the last one with medals waiting at the end.

I know I've mentioned before that my husband does not understand all the levels and nuances of skating. He is particularly clueless to my distress.

"She is leaving a champion. The world loves her, she has won more medals than most skaters can even dream of winning. Plus, she has that salad dressing commercial."

"I know, but there will be a big void now. No one can ever replace her".

"Well now you'll actually be able to watch the skating," he offers over his shoulder as he finds something to do in the laundry room.

He has never understood this emotional connection so many of us have with Michelle Kwan's skating. My eyes well up when she steps on the ice. My hands cover my face, leaving small slits like the ones in the walls of castles, when she starts her backward crossovers, glide, and then full coverage of the eyes when she goes into a jump — hold the breath, wait for the sound of the crowd or Dick Button's voice before opening. It is a long four minutes.

Has there ever been any performance more emotional than the "Field of Dreams" exhibition after the Salt Lake Olympics. That was so sad I felt like going to read "Where the Red Fern Grows" to cheer up. I can't even look at gold dresses since then.

My daughter is also a bit bewildered by all of this. She is also a big fan, but it has recently occurred to be me that I might be a bit on the effusive side of most things in my life. She has a signed skate, books, and several photos with Michelle from back-stage passes to events. (I now regret that I am not in any of the pictures and I fear the opportunity may be lost forever.)

Anyway, she asked me if I get that nervous when she skates.

I had to think about it. Do I get Michelle Kwan nervous?

Well, I often feel like leaving the building and not watching, because it is the watching that is the hardest. The judges scores, the other skaters — nothing is as hard as watching your child out on the ice doing what seems to be an impossibility: dancing on two little sharpened blades of steel on slippery ice. I mean, I think the concept is a violation of the Geneva Convention.

I also feel like I have eaten an entire tub of buttered popcorn and the family size box of Milk Duds, on top of a garlic shrimp scampi dinner *and* been on the Tilt-o-whirl, when my daughter is on the ice.

I'm afraid to look, afraid not to look in case she glances up and notices that I have my hands wrapped around the neck of the stranger in front of me. Yes, I often have to pass myself off as a traveling masseuse.

I have to look calm.

But do I get more nervous watching my daughter skate than watching Michelle Kwan skate?

"Yes," I say in one of those epiphany moments when you realize it is the only answer you can give.

I truly believe we are all given five or six — depending on how many times your own mother goes on a diet — free passes to "lie" with the small "l." You have to use them judiciously because there will be many more occasions in life when you will be tempted, but these will be "charged against you" on your Karma National Bank Visa.

Just to keep the world in balance, I ask my daughter, "Do you think I am as attractive as the mom on "According to Jim."

She smiles, "Prettier."

Ah, she has four passes left.

Selling for Beans

I am not one of those people who sits for hours on the internet.

Okay. I do check USFSA and Ice-dance. Everyday. Well, several times a day. And occasionally I visit, or "walk by" the other message boards. But, I don't have a MySpace, I don't play Mah-jongg, and I don't visit chat rooms.

Unfortunately, I have an eBay account.

My eBay account is actually connected to evolution, so I guess in some circles I could say that it is scientific.

Here is how it started. Remember a decade ago when Ty started selling those cute little stuffed animals for $4.95? Right.

Beanie Babies.

Everything was wonderful, the kids each had one, without tags of course, because they get in the way and we initially thought they were merely toys.

And then someone decided they were more valuable with tags, and that the entire American population needed to start an Ark of Beanie Babies.

Well, at least I had to. I had two children.

Looking back, the kids would have been happy with just Weenie the dog and Tusk the Walrus. But I started collecting them. For the kids.

Each day became a small animal pursuit. Card stores were called, toy stores were combed, department stores were staked out, waiting for shipments to arrive. Eventually I just started following the UPS delivery truck through the business section of our town.

Then Ty came up with one of best examples of marketing I have ever witnessed. They started selling lists, and books of lists of all of the Beanie Babies. Collectors could check them off as they found and adopted these two-ounce bundles of fluff.

Every month a new species was created.

Every month I had more blank boxes beside the unobtainable plush phantoms on my growing list.

This is how eBay evolved, or at least, this is how I remember it. This small online auction house exploded with the demand of the five-inch stuffed "friends," and $4.95 became as scarce as the dollar gallon of gas. Hundreds of collectors invested in obtaining Garcia, Cranberry, Righty, and Lefty, and whatever that white seal's name was. Actuaries predicted that some of these plush babies would sell for several thousand dollars; there seemed no end in sight. Beanies sold for whatever the market would "bear."

But, like junk bonds, the end was right in front of us.

Unfortunately, we all ran out of shelf space. And storage boxes. It seemed to happen at the same moment for everyone, although I missed the news headline that claimed homes were being insulated with the small Beanie friends.

Now, years later, I still look on eBay to see how many collectors are still holding on to the dream that there might still be a buyer for a special edition Birthday Bear.

I am left with two bins of Beanie Babies and an active eBay account.

Sometimes I toss a few of the plush pretties on the ice at Lake Placid — a Princess Di Bear here, a Peace Bear there. Sometimes other mothers turn when they see the purple and tie-dyed legs airborne and we make eye contact, and for a moment, yes, one brief moment, no words need to spoken.

It is a shared bond of painful memories: too many happy meals purchased trying to get the miniature bears, the tag that came off of the elephant, arriving five minutes too late for the last order of the month at the toy store.

No matter that eBay buyers now snub the tiny Ty treasures. I still have my Garcia Bear in my dining room china cabinet. He sits next to my set of Waterford wine glasses, and although I know some people find it odd to see him perched there, a bear in a china shop so to speak, I know the truth.

He cost more than the wine glasses.

Numbers Game

My niece is getting married in two weeks and her fiancé has planned a secret honeymoon location. Unfortunately, I figured it out in 3 1/5 minutes. He was amazed at my seemingly untrained ability.

"That was like getting medicine from a travel pack," I told him. "You have to remember, my daughter skates."

He looked at me like I was trying to eat Jell-O with a toothpick, but I know you understand.

Every September we all play the Sectional Merry-go-Round, or what region is this team skating in, twenty questions game. And, we are all a bit anxious to find out where everyone is going.

More than just idle curiosity.

Oh yes, the facts back me up.

Fact: there are 16,074 hits for the Junior section of Icedance.com with only 123 posts. Novice has 9,827 hits with 65 posts, Intermediate has 6,034 hits with 39 posts and Senior has 7,135 hits with 33 posts.

I think the senator from my district didn't get this many votes in the general election. With half of these Chris Daughtry would have been this year's American Idol winner and selling Ford Mustangs.

We all peruse the messages boards searching for clues. We print out copies and use lemon water and Q-tips looking

Sherry Bosley | 107

for hints hidden in invisible ink. We have cryptologists put in entries looking for codes. Does this message use more E's, or more W's or M's — ah, the subconscious at work.

Now here is the really odd thing. Entries had to be in last Friday; 40,000 hits on the various levels, but still no one is talking.

Just looking.

Daphne Backman, who owns, and designs for Ice-dance.com, should put a counter on, to see how many people sign on to find out if there are any new postings on the subject, then move on to one of the other boards when they see there are not.

Suspense is a good thing. We are all waiting to see if Meredith picks McDreamy or the Vet, we are waiting to see if the third Pirates of the Caribbean movie is as popular as the first one, and we are waiting to see if the OD for next year is country – Hank Williams Jr. country – or folk country – Hungarian polka etc.

Either way, I can't wait for the costumes.

But there is no reason for suspense in the sectional shuffle.

This is not a compulsory dance. It is voluntary.

I am imagining that eventually the USFSA will just have teams go to the closest section and take the top twelve scores from across the country. It would ease some of the tension.

Of course, some sections might hold out for a few days before reporting their numbers.

My Space

  Teens today have their own place to release stress and to socialize. It's called MySpace, or Facebook if they are in college or just too cool for the starter program.

  I think parents need their own venue also.

  We can call it IneedMySpace, if we have children under 18, or Doyouremembermyface if they are over 18.

  Seriously, it will be fun.

  For the IneedMySpace site, we can post all the silly faces and whiney things our children say through the years. Instead of listing how many friends we have, we can list how many tirades and rolled eyes we get in a six-year teenage life span. Other parents can go on line and commiserate and console.

  For the Doyouremembermyface site we can post current photos of ourselves behind depictions of moving twenty dollar bills that your child has to click on in a three-second period of time in order to activate the debit card in his wallet. Or perhaps a match game where your child has to match the current hair style you sport, or identify your eye color in a bonus round.

  Today was a holiday and I did not spend it with my daughter.

  She had to skate and then attend an afternoon cookout, and then dinner with friends. I called her twice because I wanted to make sure she was safely at each stage of the day (There is holiday traffic!) and then just to see how her dining experiences were going. (Hey, I take that whole "Do you know where your kids are" very seriously and, really, parents cannot be considered stalkers.)

She didn't reciprocate.

If she had, I would have told her we had left-over cole slaw and teriyaki chicken on the grill. We even used the bamboo placemats and napkins we bought in New York. I was trying to wait for her to join us, but it is now past Labor Day, so no white shoes or rattan on the patio.

So, I didn't want to call her a third time to see if she was in for the night because that might seem a bit, well, excessive. And I didn't want to make the board again.

Ah, the board!

The board is in her kitchen. She and her roommate write down on a chalkboard unusual things that people say. The problem is that most, or all, of the entries are things that I, or the other mom, have said.

Now this is a bit like politics. You know you can't take things out of context or it changes the whole meaning or slants the picture so to speak.

So, right on the board it says very clearly in yellow chalk:

"The Tin Man Didn't Have Private Parts" Mombo 6/20/06

Now, I feel very confident that I can prove this observation without everyone watching hours of the Wizard of Oz. But still, some people, probably not parents, might wonder how this could ever have entered into a conversation.

It was actually very logical. We were discussing maintenance and taking care of hinges and vital parts. But, truly, if I had not explained, you might have been left wondering.

Anyway, since I didn't want to "make the board" again, I didn't want to make another call, so I thought I would check her MySpace page, and see if she had "checked in." (Police departments have suggested that parents monitor these online accounts to make sure their children are not putting too much information on line.) I was comforted to observe that she had checked in and miffed to realize that this was her first line of "reaching out and touching someone." So that you don't worry, I never go past her opening page other than looking at her photos. I don't read her messages or even turn up the sound for the song she has attached. I mean, she needs some privacy, which, by the way, she has on Facebook, because parents can't check that unless they enroll as an undergraduate.

So, Daphne will need to free up some web space at Icedance.com to work on this Doyouremembermyface.com idea, but I believe if it is attached to a PayPal credit account for our children, we might get some hits and cognitive awareness.

We might even be able to recycle some of their old free dance programs as songs for our home page.

Pilar Bosley and John Corona compete at Nationals

Fruit of My Labor

Labor Day was created about seventy-five years ago to celebrate and recognize the contribution of the everyday worker. Initially there were parades and small town festivities to mark the efforts of the common Joe or Josephine.

We have let this tradition slip a bit, as we have almost all of the holidays not marked by a specific section in Hallmark. Now, we use it as a "recovery" day, or an extended shopping day.

Athletes use it as an opportunity to get a little more practice in, as usual.

My daughter is rising at 5:00 a.m. to go skate at a neighboring rink, because all the regular rinks are closed because of the holiday. So, on a three-day weekend, she is getting up before the sun and driving in the pre-dawn hour to go to a rink 45 minutes away.

Here is the scary thing; she doesn't even drink coffee.

Exactly! She does this cold turkey without any stimulation besides determination. Okay, she may drink a lemon Propel or the red Gatorade, but no Java pumps through those veins.

So, I ask her.

"Tomorrow is a holiday. All of the rinks are closed. Why are you skating?" (You have to keep it pretty straightforward to those who don't understand the popularity of Starbucks.)

"Because it's a training day. We're supposed to treat this as a job. Our job. We can't take off." (She tries not to use too many compound words because she thinks I'm a little too wired from drinking several cups of coffee.)

"Monday is Labor Day. The day those who labor take off. That's why the other rinks are closed."

She looks at me like I've proposed a hospital strike with picket lines.

"We can't take off. We have to skate."

I try to imagine myself feeling this strongly about my job. Feeling so dedicated that I would make myself – no, not just that – that I would *want* to go in on a holiday that I can legitimately take off. I get a little light-headed and dizzy for a moment at the thought and pour myself a third cup of coffee and add the new chocolate caramel creamer. My daughter tries to keep an impassive expression, but I can tell she is appalled, like I'm an addict or something.

"It's one day," I try to coerce her.

"Exactly. One whole day," she says firmly, picking up the creamer bottle and reading the label.

"Everyone needs a break, you never take a break."

She pushes the bottle away, and looks at me without replying.

For a moment I think she might be planning a twelve-step program for me. My voice may have been a bit higher than usual, but it is because of the pollen count this time of year and not the caffeine. I think all of this in my head, but only tell her my last thought of this reasoning process.

"It's August."

"Actually, it's September mom."

She goes over and turns off the coffeepot, and my heart does one of those double beats and as I'm tapping my fingers to keep up. I have to add the extra measures.

"Mom, maybe you should take a day off from drinking coffee. One day."

This is such a Freaky-Friday moment that I try to stop looking from my cup to the pot, wondering if she will let me top off my mug before the magic black liquid cools.

"I don't need to drink coffee. I just like the smell. I don't need it."

"Remember last year when you had to get a blood test and you stopped at the WaWa before going in so the cup would be ready when you came out from the doctor?"

"Don't be ridiculous, I was just early and wanted to save time afterward. So I could get to work faster."

"Ummm. Why don't you come with me to the rink tomorrow and walk around the building outside while I skate? You could have an apple juice instead."

I cover my mouth so she doesn't see my almost gagging reflex.

"I would, but it is a holiday tomorrow. I know the youth of today do not take the time to reflect on what it means, but some of us must preserve the traditions."

She comes over and gives me a hug, but I suspect she is checking my heart rate, which of course has risen because I stood up.

"Okay, good night. I hope you sleep well."

She is such a considerate child. She knows I suffer bouts of insomnia because I worry so much about her and all the hours she puts in.

Some things are just not healthy.

Family Matters

Six months ago, while having a Hallmark moment, I decided to have a family reunion, blending both sides of the family into a serene afternoon of bliss, benevolence, and bounty. This would be my side of the family, from the south, and my husband's side of the family from the north. Together. At our house.

You might ask what I was drinking in March to bring about this obvious loss of reason. I will tell you that it was not due to any alcoholic elixir, but to the sense of "skating guilt."

You all know what I mean. You miss Aunt Betty's birthday, and your cousin's anniversary bash, and one of your second cousins once-removed baby showers. Weekends are always tied up with skating practice, traveling, training, and competitions.

And sometimes you said there were events even when there weren't, just to get out of eating cole slaw, deviled eggs, and store-bought cake while someone opened presents like they were going to re-use the wrapping paper, bows, and scotch tape for the war effort.

Relatives are always understanding. After all, they have added all the facts together, multiplied the time spent skating, subtracted the money probably used (they are always off of course), and divided the miles to come up with the only answer that makes sense to them:

"Oh, she is going to be an Olympian one day."

No matter how improbable this would be, they don't understand. When you tell them she doesn't even think of that, they just stare at you blankly, like you only went to the buffet table one time. When you try to explain the chances are greater that someone will finally figure out the real plot to "Lost," or that you will be the next "American Idol" they just guffaw, and say, "Oh, stop being so modest. She's got to be a star, look at that smile in those skating pictures."

So, we gave up trying to explain the hierarchy of skating and setting realistic goals. We compromise by saying, "Well, we'll just see where it goes" to their "We already know where she's going!"

So of course, I feel a bit guilty occasionally. Hence, the family reunion at our abode.

The problem is, each side of the family wants to be right all of the time. It is like having all the teams out on the warm-up and no skating order. It is chaos.

They argue points about everything.

Which football team is better, the Steelers or the Eagles.

Which baseball team is better, the Cubs or the Yankees.

Which soda has the best taste, Coke or Pepsi.

I think you get the gist of the conversation. Each side claims the grandchildren by some twisted version of the Immaculate Conception, thereby making all genetic material the side with that family's birth name.

So now that we are on the eve of the event, we sit like zombies with inviter's remorse.

My son asks if he has to stay the entire time.

"Of course. This is your family," I admonish.

"I'm not looking at any more surgery scars," he announces.

My daughter joins in the discussion.

"If they start again about bladder infections, I'm pleading a headache and going upstairs."

"Don't be ridiculous," I advise. "That would never work.

We'll have to pretend they called you to the rink for an emergency practice session. You know, for the future of the red, white, and blue."

Will Work for Shoes

There are days I question my chosen profession.

I love the written word, so I thought it would be exciting to share the joy of unwrapping an author's tone and the mysteries of theme and style to the youth of today. Unfortunately, Shakespeare does not have a MySpace. Canterbury Tales is not an iPod selection. Essays cannot be text-messaged.

I am fortunate to have another income that keeps me above the ramen noodle eating level that accompanies my job. This is another one of those shifts in the universe of logical thinking. Teachers must have a bachelor's degree although most have a master's. I, and about 25 percent of my peers, have an additional 30 credits (this is actually worth about the same as having the edges finished on skating costumes — no one cares from fifteen feet away). Teachers only get bonuses on their Staples Rewards card.

Today in the newspaper I read where a football player for a professional team just received an $11 million bonus for becoming the starting quarterback. This is on top of his double digit (in the millions) football contract. In the business section of the same paper, there was a blurb that Raymond "Chip" Mason picked up a $14 million bonus as a reward for his work last year in the company he owns.

Discussing salaries is always a touchy subject in my house. My husband always shakes his head when I write monthly checks to coaches. He has assured me that even his doctor does not clear $85.00 to $95.00 an hour. To try to win a few points, I called a friend who was a neurologist and proffered the question. He laughed. He told me when you subtract insurance, office space rental or purchase, salary requirements for office personnel and associates, and factor in the cost of medical school and loss of 10 years of earning power, he was lucky to clear half of that amount.

I, of course, didn't tell my husband he was correct.

My husband also just shakes his head after each competition when we all come home, regroup, change choreography, and re-tool the programs.

"We are just tweaking it," I say.

"Really," he says in disbelief. "Because it looks like they are changing entire sections that some would say were given to you at 'expert fees' the first time."

"Skating is very fluid," I answer. Sometimes it is hard to discuss the technical components to those on the outside.

"I see. Well, speaking of fluid. When the plumber came last week to fix the pipe in the bathroom, you were appalled that he charged $65.00 an hour. And he went to school for his profession. And I bet if the water started backing up, or had some reduced pressure and he had to come out again, you wouldn't expect him to charge you a second time would you? Or maybe bring in a specialist to turn on the water and watch it run. You know, tweak it, or watch it to see if it needs tweaking."

I think you see why I try not to discuss the complexities of skating with my husband.

So my daughter is on the threshold of deciding what she wants to do "after skating."

My husband is no help here. Why send her to college he asks. She can become a coach and buy us a beach house in Myrtle Beach with her Christmas bonuses. (Wow, I thought he didn't know about the coach bonuses!)

I, of course, take my parenting role a little more seriously sometimes than he. I try to offer my daughter real life advice.

"It is really very simple," I tell her. "In life you need to make enough money to do, or have, the things in life that matter. Some people find that in a job, some people find a job that pays them enough to do the things they love when they are not working."

She looks at me blankly, so I break it down for her.

"Sweetheart, you have to decide how many pair of shoes you want to buy a year. If you don't care and can live with one or two pair, you will go into a service field. Otherwise, look at the Fortune 500 list and plan."

She pales at thought of two pairs of shoes annually and starts looking seriously at her college course catalogs.

"Well", she said, "If nothing else, I could always coach."

Pilar in the gold waltz dress, or "She's wearing my BMW."

Mother's Day

My daughter and the rest of the skating group spent the weekend in Buffalo, New York, discussing all the things that "move" U.S. figure skating.

While she was dining and dancing in the company of Kristi Yamaguchi, I was at home discovering the joys of the new and enhanced Lysol toilet bowl cleaner. It's not that I am bitter or jealous, it is just that I wonder when this baton pass took place — where my children live such enriched and exciting lives, while I am home taking lint out of the dryer vent.

And I know I am not alone in this: Charlie White's mom mentioned she had the raucous outing of buying kitty litter this weekend while he and Meryl delivered speeches and signed autographs at the conference.

As a parent of any athlete, you assume the role of spectator. There is a period of time, however, when you actually believe you fulfill a vital role in the triumvirate of athlete, coach, parent. You believe you actually help chart the course and make the decisions. As a parent you feel you navigate the rough water of hard choices in addition to paying the bills.

Once my daughter started driving, a crack opened in this logic, much like when you own a small percentage of shares in a corporation and you get to "vote" on the annual report. I used to spend hours in music stores, listening to possible choices for skating music, only to be told, "Joe Cocker's voice is too gravely," "Tom Jones is too 'panties on the stage,'" "Bryan Adams has no change in tempo." Every year, one team or another skates to one of my former offerings, and my daughter says, "Oh, we almost skated to that, remember?"

This makes my eye start to twitch in the right corner.

The role of spectator is not an unpleasant one. You drive, you wait, you watch. You commiserate with other parents. You cheer. You cry.

Yesterday, on my mission to purchase the long lasting cleaning agent (buy one, get one free), I passed a softball field of what looked like 10- to 12-year-old girls. I saw a father behind the fence at home plate wearing an orange shirt (no real explanation for this as the team was wearing Carolina blue) and striped shorts — the bottom of a postal worker's uniform. This is typical of any child athlete's parents: being able to transition from one life form to another in a moment's notice — leaving work to instantly engage in the sport of spectating.

And so, there is a part of me that truly misses those days: the 150-mile commute to a training rink, the lunch or dinner box packing, juggling keeping skates sharpened, yet not interfering with training. The sitting. The waiting. The watching.

Now, I am mostly in the stage of hearing.

As in, I "hear" about what is happening.

Of course, this is filtered, I am sure, as much as a White House press secretary's news conference.

"My alarm didn't go off this morning" translates in real speech as "I stayed out late and probably turned off my alarm and had to jump in my clothes, throw everything in a suitcase and catch the 4:00 a.m. shuttle to the airport."

"Kristi Yamaguchi is so tiny and pretty" translates in real speech to mean that she will never shop in the plus-size department and that she is pretty. Some facts are universal in any language.

"It was really exciting and we got a lot done" means there were productive meetings and afterwards groups went out until 2:00 a.m. and had fun. I believe the current era Karaoke equivalent is a quiz game of some sort that may or may not have been played. (In which case my daughter has a slight handicap in that she becomes Jessica Simpson in the category of geography.)

As Mother's Day approaches, I would like to remind all of the athletes in the world:

1. Take a few moments to remember who has had your back, because they have been in the background watching, wishing, and waiting.

2. Don't buy your mom cleaning supplies or kitty litter. We already have that area covered.

Bedazzled Canucks

Canada has issued a plan to bring in more television viewers for the 2010 Olympics to be hosted in Vancouver this winter: make the male athletes in figure skating appear more "Macho."

In a world that seems to have lost many of the standard methods of operation, where we are bailing out businesses for failing to use due caution and then watching that money be doled out to the very executives who squandered the capital in the first place, this may make sense. But to those who are actively engaged in the sport, it is another albatross to be thrown at a genre that is trying to maintain the dignity and grace that defines it.

"Perhaps," proffers the executives who are hoping for lucrative commercial sales, "we could tone down the glitter and sparkles on the male figure skating costumes to emote a more masculine image. Perhaps we can promote the serious training regimen that goes into becoming an elite skater."

What they would really like it seems, is to somehow makeover the sport into some type of extreme competition, perhaps using a canon to fire those unused crystals and beading onto the ice so the skaters have to dodge and dive to avoid calamity. What they would have us believe is that we no longer have an audience that can appreciate the haunting notes of a classic violin, or the penned craftsmanship of Eliot, or the muted pastels of Monet.

There are fewer inductees into "I love figure skating" club of faithful watchers and followers. If figure skating could Tweet, it would seemingly have fewer followers than snowboarding, cage fighting, and, if it is to be believed, Fly-dog competitions.

So the camera is hoping to pan the ice surface covered with James Dean types: Levis, white t-shirts, a pocket that perhaps has the imprint of a Skoal can. Austrian crystals and one-piece velour jumpsuits will take on the persona of a crying baby or a ringing cell phone in a five-star restaurant.

All of this, of course, in the hopes of getting the viewing attention of the 15- to 25-year-old male who has previously been engrossed in the twists and turns of the half-pipe.

If Canada had bothered to call, we could have told them this is the wrong tactic. Young Paul Bunyons, driving Dodge PowerWagons with mounted gun racks are never going to turn by choice to an ice skating competition and clamber about the degree of difficulty of a triple axel or the intricate footwork within any program.

They will, however, watch it if their girlfriends are controlling the remote.

Let's be honest, how many men go voluntarily to see any movie that has Reese Witherspoon or Jennifer Aniston in the leading role? Yet, these are box office smash hits for six or seven weeks. The rugged males who would deny crying at *Marley and Me* are the same ones who will be sitting on the couch in late winter with their significant other, watching Johnny, Evan, Jeremy, and Adam dazzle a sold-out crowd in the northwest mountains.

Canada could salvage the moment, from their perspective anyway, by putting rugged "macho" ads in the commercial breaks, perhaps giving those with way too much testosterone something to look forward to. A chainsaw ad here, a steel-toed boot ad there, and maybe some footage of ice-road trucking. It is what executives try to garner all the time: a win-win situation.

What will not work for the millions of current ice skating fans is the concept of trying to change what we love about the sport. We love the dramatic music. We love the sparkle. We love the pizzazz.

Maybe Canada should take the opposite approach. Instead of worrying about trying to make ice-skating more "Macho," they should try to develop the sensitive side of the nonskating male population. They could start by requiring those with male chromosomes to read a trio of Nicholas Sparks novels, watch the first season of Grey's Anatomy, and go to a local spa for a pedicure.

Right before the Olympics, the Canucks could bedazzle their hockey uniforms and maybe go with the velvet practice pants.

It's an option, anyway.

Second Sunday in May

Mother's Day is the annual calendar mark of our lives, when we take stock of our progresses and processes.

This year was a bit melancholy for me; my son is away at college studying for finals, and my daughter is out of the country having a much-deserved vacation. My husband tried to fill the void by making raspberry and white chocolate pancakes for breakfast and offering me cards from the dogs and the cats. This would have had a better outcome if one of the cats had allowed me sleep past 5:30 a.m., and if Izzy would have left me to linger over coffee without the constant eardrum-shattering bark reminder to throw her Wubba.

This was a year that, as a mother, I realize I have not had an opportunity to do much "mothering." Both of my children are making their own decisions, plotting their own courses, and hitching their wagons to their selected distant stars. The only thing they get from me is the daily reminder to "stay safe," "be aware of your surroundings," and "do you have to buy the whole album from iTunes? Couldn't you just select a few songs?" After all, this independence is still paid for by me.

Because of my mothering-once-removed status, I have asked my daughter at least to come to my aid if she sees me doing something odd or out of character.

She is to intercede if she discovers, for example, that I am on a first name basis with the FedEx man because I am doing 3 a.m. shopping with either QVC or the Home Shopping Network.

She is to raid my closet and take me to the nearest Chico's if she notices I am wearing one of those smock-type aprons that snap in the front, or, if I start carrying a Kate Spade knock-off with a glued on label.

She is to open a can of Betty Crocker's Milk Chocolate Frosting and hold it under my nose if she ever sees me lingering over an ad for any footwear made by Croc's, regardless of color, style, or on-sale status.

So, with her in Mexico, and me feeling a bit Willie Nelson-ish (Mama Don't Let Your Children Grow Up to be Outlaws), it is probably understandable that I had a breakdown on Friday night at my monthly Bunko game. On the second Friday of each month, sixteen of us meet and hurl pink dice while drinking wine and snacking on Kailua dip and theme cake. We shout "Bunko" and "Babies" and ring bells, and by the end of the night we are all in our happy zones. This month doubled as a baby shower for one of our younger members who is pregnant with her second child.

The best thing I gave her was actually the message I placed in her card — "Good Luck. Don't forget to only look at Rec League Sports!" — I had eaten my 10th Kailua dipped strawberry, and I felt a wave of sadness ebb up about how quickly the time goes when I dropped my napkin. While retrieving it, I noticed that three of my fellow Bunkoettes had on the aforementioned Croc footwear.

I was stunned.

I mean, what could I say? It's not as if they are stylish or attractive. They look like miniature clown shoes.

So, as a diplomatic displaced mother, I asked, "Why do you wear those?"

They pounced on me like the only attendee at an Amway party.

I was given the testimonials: They are so comfortable; they massage the feet; there is never an offensive odor.

I accepted an offer to wear a pair around the room. I liked the feel. I liked the clunky oddness and the rubber "gellin" padding. I liked the in-your-face color attacks of the pinks and purples.

I capitulated. I conceded. I converted.

I wanted to go to Dick's Sporting Goods at 10:30 and buy a pair but was forced to wait and make an on-line purchase at midnight. (Please. This is very different than QVC shopping.)

And now I wait.

For my son to come home from his first year of college. For my daughter to get off the plane, looking tanned and rested.

For my Croc's to arrive FedEx Express.

I will need to distract my daughter from my new footwear selection, and I think I have found that vehicle. I have to call Ann Greenthal, organizer extratonaire of the Lake Placid Ice Dancing Championships and a few other ladies, whom I will need to organize some regional branches of MSST, or what I am tentatively calling Mothers of Skaters Syncho Team. The concept is simple. We skater moms (and dads) will choreograph and skate to six-minute programs where we use artistic concepts and skill to present a group medley of our children's free dance from the previous year. With the focus on adult skating I think this is truly the bridge program.

If we can pull this off by Lake Placid, there won't be a dry eye in the house. This will be great, since Croc's are supposed to be good in wet weather.

Getting the Time of Day

Since this is Cupid's week, I suppose some people would expect me to wax poetic about the anomalies of our heartfest holiday. And I probably would except for the ticking of the clock by my desk (true, there is a bowl of pink and red peanut M&Ms in front of it, but I'm ignoring that for the common good).

All of my clocks are set on Eastern Standard Time. They are as accurate as possible, since, to me, that seems to be the point of having a sensitive time piece.

Unfortunately, my spouse and, alas, my daughter live in an altered time zone, one that I have discovered is inhabited by a huge percentage of our populace. In fact, the numbers are as close as the Clinton-Obama delegate count. There are those who live on "real time" and those who live on, well, let's call it what it is: "fake time".

My husband and daughter survive and navigate the rooms of our lives by a series of altered clocks that are as complicated as navigating the Panama Canal in an oil freighter.

The bedroom alarm clock is eight minutes fast.

The microwave time reads five minutes ahead of reality.

The Bose boasts a four-minute head start.

"Why do you do this?" I ask them.

And I get the look. The look that all clock defacers give to nondefacers. It's probably how smokers look at nonsmokers who fan toxic clouds out of their pathways.

"Because it gives us more time!" They respond as if they are writing the introduction to *The Dummies Guide to Changing Time*.

I know I shouldn't, but I do. I try to reason with them.

"How does it give you more time?"

"Because, when the alarm goes off in the morning, I know that I can turn it off and I still have eight more minutes to stay in bed."

"So why don't you set the clock for 5:22 and know that you can just stay in bed until 5:30."

They shake their heads. They look at me with pity.

"You don't get it."

No. No, I don't. I am forced to disregard any clock in my home that is not set by a central control, like Comcast and Verizon, the only sane source of digital imaging in my home. The others haunt me like constant versions of Liar's Poker, chiming and bonging at odd moments of the day and night, Ave Maria going off at 5:10, Westminster Chimes at 3:13, some as much as twenty minutes off the mark.

Today, I went to the train station to pick up my daughter, and I drove her car, thereby using her gas. I had a few errands to run, and I was running a bit late, so I was happy to pull into the small station and see no one waiting on the platform. I thought it odd when the waiting passengers starting arriving fifteen minutes after the train was to pull in, as if they had advance notice there had been a delay.

When my daughter eventually arrived I asked if they had been behind schedule in Washington.

"No, we were a few minutes early actually."

I looked at her clock on the dashboard, flashing valentine red numbers. Ahh.

Et tu, RAV4.

"Just tell me why you set your car clock ahead. You're already dressed and in the car, so you're on your way. Why can't you be on real time when you're driving?"

"Because it gives me more time. I can stop for a coffee or a bagel."

I cannot respond to this, because, well, there is no response. I can only speculate on the huge consumer market that exists untapped as yet: calendars with Tax Day marked as April 5, Labor Day on the last Monday in August, July 4 being bracketed with fireworks graphics on June 27.

April 1 would of course have to remain as it is.

No one should forget the day we honor fools.

Three Questions

There seems to be a plethora of dot com businesses out there that specialize in finding people who are compatible with each other. Sometimes this a dating service, often it is an employment program, or the new genre of "finding friends."

For those of us who grew up talking on a Princess rotary phone, this seems a bit off the mark. In reality, all of us could come up with three questions that would determine if someone could be a life partner or a BFF. It really is that simple. The difficulty is (a) we didn't ask the questions, or (b) we asked them but decided to overlook their answers.

For example, my first question would be, "Do you like animals." This is a deal breaker. The response must be yes. Not "Yes, particularly with A-1 sauce," but a yes followed by some vignette about a childhood or current pooch. People cannot coexist who do not share the joy of dog ownership, be-damn the hair and muddy feet on occasion.

My next question would be, "How many chemistry classes did you take in college?" The correct answer here would be "one or less," followed by a long shudder. If they answer "three" or "Does bio-chem count?" I know there would be communication issues. This is a person who will use logic to the third power and analyze things that should just be enjoyed for the mere spirit or tone. So even if they answered yes to the first question, they would never hold a birthday party for said pet, or have three different call names for their dog. Their dog would, in fact, be named after an element found on the periodic table or perhaps an enzyme.

My third question would have to do with ice-skating. It would be, "Do you believe ice-skating is a sport?"

This is tricky. You may have to consider the hesitation factor. Most definitely parlay their answer with some tricky counter questioning.

"Do you mean like in the Olympics?"

Yes, but even if the skater isn't going to the Olympics.

"Do you mean ladies or men?"

That is a curb kicker; overlap here would carry over in so many areas.

"Well, maybe in Asia. They seem to excel in this arena."

Please, some of you can imagine why this sends me to the snack bar or exit door.

"Do you mean as in hockey?" No, no pucks are involved. No striped referee uniforms, just your basic crossovers and three-turns into a jump or lift.

"Do you mean where they wear all those sparkly gee-gads and make-up?"

Yes—it is the equivalent of black marker under the eyes for baseball players and the 97 tattoos on each NFL member.

These are the questions that should be asked for my particular mission in life, perhaps others could be added, but the outcome would not change.

In hindsight, I should have asked my husband what temperature he likes to keep the thermostat set, or does it really matter which way the paper towels go on the holder, or is it really irreparable if I put my foot on the threshold of the car door. I should have asked, but I did not.

Maybe all of those fables and tales where the genie grants three wishes were wrong; maybe they should have granted three questions.

Stretching Fiction

We are into the "Dog Days of Summer" although recently I am not sure if this should not read "Daze."

The highlight of each day seems to center on if I should have Honey-Nut Cheerios or settle for the more sensible plain, whole-grain variety.

My son, home for the summer from his freshman year at college, announced last week that he wanted to spend an afternoon with me for some "quality time." I packed a travel package of Kleenex for our outing and my new Cool-pix camera, anticipating in-depth conversations and photo-ops at the city museum. "Quality time" to an 18-year-old turns out to be a stop at the local running-shoe store for new Asics ($132.00), a haul from Office Depot for second year school supplies ($84.00), and a jaunt through the aisles of Target ($76.00). We had more of a Saturday Night Live spoof for a MasterCard commercial than soul searching mutual discovery. It was, however, time with my son, who will now deny that he ever skated, let alone had the leading role in the ice version of "Peter and the Wolf, an off-Broadway production to say the least.

As usual, the high drama in my daily existence is anchored to my daughter and all things skating.

My aforementioned promise to my daughter to complete a novel this summer has been productive. It is a work of fiction, but some truth may have layered itself into the plot and characterizations.

"Mom, you Cannot Use These Names!" my daughter editorializes from the bottom of page three.

"They are just working names; it helps me keep things in order. Brock was actually a name from a popular soap-opera. I think he was a bit of a cad for at least one season, but may have redeemed himself; I'm not sure, I stopped watching."

"Don't you think it is a bit drastic to have the murder plot center around the three positions for the Olympic team? Is that going to be believable?"

"Sweetheart, it will be so believable. You were too young to remember the mother of girl who was trying out for cheerleader who killed the mom of a team member hoping the daughter would be so distraught it would open a position on the squad. In real life things are not so tight; in fiction, anyone with any sense would have realized that would not work."

My daughter looks at me with a slight elevation of her eyebrows. As she advances toward the end of her teen years, this seems to be a more fashionable conveyance of annoyance or vexation than the previously moderated eye roll. She has added more capitalization to her speech patterns however.

I try to placate her.

"I toyed with centering the plot around a costume ordered from Russia that had real diamonds smuggled in instead of the ever-glued Austrian crystals, but that seemed so, I don't know, trite and expected."

"Ummh ... well, you aren't using any character's names that might Cause Me Embarrassment, are you? You don't have minor characters with extraordinary skating abilities covertly named "Chuck Black," or "pixie" girls with oxymoron names?"

"Sweetheart, this is a work of fiction; there will be some truth to it — the training schedules, the friendships, the moms sitting in the stands. The actual sport itself will be clarified and researched. Some things have to be changed, of course. I cannot divulge the price of skating costumes or the hourly rate of skating coaches, for example. To do so might launch a horrific fluff piece regarding lycra and spandex before the Cleveland Nationals and commence an IRS investigation into unreported income, or at least padded expense accounts."

She sighs and closes the manuscript. "I think I will wait for this to come out in hard cover. When do you think this will be published?"

"I'm thinking they might wait until right before the 2010 Vancouver Games; it can be part of the pre-hyped press. Maybe it will even get a bit of play like the Harry Potter series, or the new Twilight books, oh, not in sales, of course, but that the book stores will open at midnight, and fans can come dressed in skating costumes."

"That is an image I want to erase my mind. There should be a weight restriction on lycra."

"Well, it isn't that far-fetched. Remember you went to see "Blades of Glory" a few years ago with about twenty of your fellow skaters and you were all decked out in glissenette, rhinestones, and beads."

"That was different *and* several years ago; I think we've all grown a bit since then."

"Of course you have, dear, and I would never reveal secrets like that in my novel. No one would believe it anyway."

Tree of a Thousand Suns

December is the time of year when sleigh bells ring and the scent of pine nectar fills the air with pungent fumes.

Well, except at our house.

My husband and I have been engaged in the decade-old battle of "plastic or paper"; or in the language of the holidays: real or artificial.

I have voted for "real" for twenty years. A real, live, beautifully sculpted Douglas fir, one with tiny pine cones embedded on the branches, one with the scent of a northern forest that cannot be captured by a Glade Mist candle, one that symbolizes the blend of nature and custom that is shared around the world.

My husband has opted for the fake, pole-in-a-box version of color-coded Brillo-like limbs that assemble to look as much like a Christmas tree as those black-and-white, puckered plastic knock-off handbags are supposed to look like classic Chanels.

Two years ago I got excited because my husband told me we were going to try something new for Christmas. I imagined trekking through the woods with the entire family, Izzy wearing a plaid sweater and making little paw prints in the

Sherry Bosley | 147

snow for us to follow, carting a thermos of hot cocoa and a bag of crisp Madelines, and finding the perfect Christmas tree — size, shape, smell, color — graded like a flawless diamond. We would shake off the snow and cut it down with a small handsaw, thus not disturbing the ambience of the forest setting.

My husband's comment of seemingly spontaneous action was instead a ploy to go to Sears department store to purchase a "Pre-Lit" tree.

Our new tree is seemingly powered by 5,000 Halogen Jeep headlights. On the brightness meter, the only measurable object above our tree is in fact, the Sun. One of the benefits of this is, of course, our family room is fifteen degrees warmer than the rest of the house.

I know some families gather around the Christmas tree, trimming and decorating it together, perhaps singing Christmas songs and sipping eggnog while humming along to "Granny Got Run Over by a Reindeer."

This is not the case at our house.

My husband must place each ornament on the tree because only he knows its place. The rest of us sit on the floor holding decorations in our hands with expressions much like the young boy asking for more gruel in *Oliver Twis*t: "Please sir, can I give you more."

The finished tree is dressed to the nines in an eclectic array of finery. We have Waterford and pre-school macaroni. We have dogs, ceramic angels, and painted crab shells. We have antique wax mixed with Precious Moments figurines.

And then we have the skate ornaments.

By skate ornaments, I don't mean one or two. I'm talking enough to decorate the mammoth fir in Rockefeller Square. I'm sure we never intended to acquire as many as we did, just as we never thought we would own 300 Beanie Babies, but there they are never-the-less, spotlighted by eight million candlelit beacons.

My husband takes comfort in the fact that my daughter will one day want these for her own home. But I know the truth.

Just as my son will never take the Fox Terrier when he graduates from college, my daughter will never want 600 skate ornaments for her tree.

"Why did you buy all of these?" she asks when their glass blades blind us in reflection.

"I didn't buy ALL of them," I answer, "some were gifts."

She looks at me skeptically. I turn away from her and the tree of one thousand suns. It has been rumored that I "go overboard" sometimes. This is a myth, but myths are hard to defuse. Just look at that whole King Arthur craze.

I ponder what to do with my box of skating ornaments in the years to come, and then smile at my plan. Since I cannot have a "real" tree, nor trek into the forest to collect a piney trophy of my own, I will venture forth each year to the local Christmas tree farm and anoint one special tree of my own. Instead of tagging it and cutting it down, I will hang an ice skate ornament from its boughs and some lucky family will find a partially decorated tree in the woods.

I will hereafter be known as "The Skate Fairy," no longer a myth, but a legend.

Running Circles

Today I realized I have a problem.

I'm not going to go as far as call it an addiction.

Others would disagree, I know, especially those who have tried to wean me away and offer inferior substitutions. My epiphany of comprehension came at six am when I realized that my daughter had not only borrowed my car for the week while hers is being serviced, but that I had left my work bag on the back seat. The bag that houses my DayRunner.

When I say DayRunner, picture rich, burgundy, Corinthian leather divided by well-used tabs that denote a monthly calendar, a weekly calendar, notes, contacts, and memos. Imagine the plastic sleeves that hold business cards, a fifth grade book mark drawn by my son eight years ago, a note from my then five-year old daughter using phonetic stretch spelling to express how happy she was that the "pillgrams ate terkey wth the Neightves se we culd be a happy famly." Envision an envelope that holds every ticket stub since 1984, ranging from *Spamelot* to Toby Keith to a Ravens-Steeler game.

This is the book of life to me.

I have all of my appointments on the monthly sheets and all of my notes and comments on the weekly pages.

I know what you're thinking.

Many people have moved into the current era and have Trios, Blackberries, or one of the other electronic devices that require the user to record data by using an enlarged toothpick-like instrument. The disciples of this mode would argue that these compact instruments hold limitless information in a neat and easily accessible manner.

I'll concede this point although this style is no more for me than wearing translucent plastic platform heels. I need to be able to "flip" and write in pencil, pen, or marker. I need to highlight with a color that stands out, not with a slightly lighter shade of gray; I need to be able to see the boldness of Lemon Yellow or Prom Pink.

So today I am without my planner. I do not have access to my username and passwords for approximately 50 online sites that range from my United air miles to Shop Bop to my FSU account. I cannot look back to the summer to see the total of my Lake Placid Golden Arrow hotel bill or the date I had my hair colored – ah, infused with highlights – or how many core strengthening sessions my daughter had with her trainer in October.

Some may gloat at my dependence on an archaic method of record keeping. They might try to compare my little notebook as the equivalent of a slide rule against the power of a calculator, but I would beg to differ.

All of the electronic data recording devices are missing the power and sensation of holding an artifact in your hand. There is something uplifting about holding an original document and savoring the meaning and complexities of the written word – as opposed to a typed word or, to be more specific, a stylused word.

My daughter arrived at her apartment to discover my bag of bullion in the back of her car and called to utter the words I dreaded.

"UH-OH, I have your book."

Since I had already made the discovery and practiced saying the words without much of an inflection in my voice, she was almost convinced.

"That's okay. I don't really need it."

Perhaps she heard the paper bag I had been breathing into crinkle over the phone.

"Mom, I can drive it back home or meet you half-way."

"No, don't be silly. I can wait until this week-end. It's only six days."

"I could FedEx it to you tomorrow, and you would have it Wednesday."

I consider this for a moment and then discard the idea. Ever since the movie "Castaway," I have not been too sure that every package makes it to its destination.

"No, that's okay. I'll just wait." I hoped she thought the cracking in my voice was just from the portable phone.

"Well ... if you're sure."

"It will be fine, it will be okay ..." I repeat this as a mantra to myself and to her and then I ask her for one favor.

"Would you please take it inside and then mark the days off each day? Use a dark blue marker and mark left to right — one line."

She hesitates for only a moment and then says, "Sure, no problem," and I know I have given her fodder for down time, when the zamboni makes its run the next day.

I would make a note of that in my DayRunner if I had it in hand.

Conservative Estimate

After years of fixing ice bags of frozen peas and heating rice packs in the microwave for bumps and bruises for my skater, I have been walking a bit akimbo myself with a bum knee. Instead of surgery, my doctor, who makes Dr. Quinn, medicine woman, seem like a risk taker, decided I should get physical therapy.

This basically means I enter a therapy room where I observe other patients in whirl pool tubs — a seemingly relaxing and comforting treatment — as I strap on weights and proceed to pull the equivalent of a heavy road grader across the room about forty times. I think the logic here is that so many other parts of my body will hurt that I will not be able to focus on my knee. Truthfully, I may be in the next Budweiser Super Bowl ad.

And I do this because my doctor also gives me medication that makes my knee feel fabulous, seriously fabulous. In fact, I can do an off-ice Beilman with absolutely no pain. So I knew there would be a downside to my newly discovered flexibility. I initially thought it was just going to be the Iditarod type therapy I had to endure. But I was wrong.

I developed a rash. It started on my leg and then moved to my arm. And my oh-so-conservative doctor said, "Wonder what that's all about." He then suggested I stop taking my-knee-feels-great medicine until my system "calmed down."

"Maybe it's just my body reacting to the stress and strain

Sherry Bosley | 155

of pulling several tons every other day."

"That doesn't sound probable," he answered.

"Really, because I am sweating in places I previously had no idea I had sweat glands in the near vicinity. I think my skin could be rebelling against that."

So I had to relinquish my pills. Then I was limping and breaking out in some mutant form of what looked like poison ivy with a red Mohawk.

And still my rash raged.

A phone call to Dr. No got the advice that I should take some Benadryl. So then I limped around trying not to scratch while also drinking coffee to stay awake.

No change. This time Dr. I Won't Even Wear a White Lab Coat Because It's Too Bright asked, "Have you tried anything new? New laundry soap, new sheets?"

"No, " I responded, "Other than working like a mule on the Erie Canal, nothing has changed."

"That's odd," he concluded.

"Can you prescribe something for it?"

"Well, you might be allergic to it if I did."

"Or," I retorted, "I might not be."

He finally agreed to phone in a salve that had to be mixed by the pharmacist. From his expression, it must have last been used in Mayberry.

So I think you see a pattern here. Now I am limping, sleepy, scratchy, and gooey.

I weighed my options. I could go to the Express Care office located in the next town and get a shot by a doctor who was not fazed by all the new-fangled advances in medicine, or I could resort to the home health magic that my mother used throughout my entire childhood.

In the movie "My Big Fat Greek Wedding," the audience is supposed to laugh when the father uses Windex on everything from zits to diaper rash. I didn't get the joke the first few times. This is because my own mother has a similar remedy that she has dosed us with since my first cognitive memory — no, not the sweet smelling window cleaner but full strength Listerine. And not the citrus or spearmint options either. No, this has to be the original brand that was so strong they had to pack it in a brown cardboard wrapper.

And so I bathed with a cotton ball and Listerine, berating myself as I dabbed. In truth, it took two treatments until my rash subsided to a mere pink blush upon the skin.

Two days later my doctor called. "How's the rash?"

"It's gone."

"Just as I suspected. It just needed time to run its course. I'll call in another prescription for your anti-inflammatory."

"Oh, that's okay. My knee is feeling much better also."

Of course, I'll never know if it was because I stopped my torturous regime or because I dabbed some Listerine on my patella each night.

"This will fit in the overhead," while traveling to JGP in Germany

When Worlds Collide

So, odd things happen when worlds collide.

This, of course, means the skating world and the "other" world.

My daughter was on vacation last week in California. This was the first time she has been on a plane in five years that did not require her to pack her skates and have her carry-on filled with four competition dresses, which are always scrutinized at customs as if we are potential diamond smugglers.

Them: "What are these costumes used for again?"

Me: "She is an ice dancer, she wears these for competitions."

Them: "It just seems odd. There is not much fabric, and the ice is so very cold. Why do you need all these doo-dads? There are more of them than fabric."

Me: "It just helps accentuate the dance. They're just crystals really, merely ornamental."

Them: "And yet you hold them so tightly, as if they are worth thousands of dollars."

So my daughter got to travel very light this trip, no skates and no mom, just a VISA, platinum edition. By Tuesday, I was beginning to realize how all of those people must feel who get postcards from their traveling garden gnome. I was getting phone calls about all the adventures of my little plastic pledge card.

"Mom, guess where I am?"

"You're sitting at the beach watching big waves?"

"No! I'm sitting in a restaurant in the Beverly Hills Hotel."

"That's nice," I reply as I sip my can of Campbell's Creamy Tomato Soup-to-Go.

"No, it's awesome. I'm just killing time until my 5:00 appointment at LA Ink. They have a two hundred dollar minimum there, does that sound right?"

She asks me this not because I am a tattoo expert, but because she is aware that her perception of costs has been skewed or warped a bit, like a DVD that has been left in the sun on the dashboard, because of skating.

In her skating world it is normal to pay a few thousand dollars for a dress she might only wear four or five times, so does it not make sense to buy jeans that ring up at $250.00 when you can wear them forever.

In her skating world it is normal to pay $1,200.00 for a pair of boots and blades that might hold up for six to eight months, so why is it not practical to buy a pair of Christian Louboutin pumps and Tory Burch sandals that will last several seasons.

In her skating world it is normal to pay some coaches two dollars a minute for their time (even when the first 10 minutes of a lesson is just warming up, which means literally I hand over a twenty dollar bill to have them say, "Go stroke."), so is it not reasonable that a tattoo artist can charge even more for their artistic needle carving.

I hesitate before answering her.

I know she is only getting a small, miniscule piece of art that is symbolic and very special to her. It probably would not take more than fifteen minutes to complete. The only other option is to allow them to fill up the minimum price with vines, or flowers, or angel wings. Do I dare think she would get a little token "Mom" engraved on the top of her foot?

I shake my head and bring myself back to reality.

"It's okay, sweetheart. It's like when you have a lesson and you aren't feeling great that day. You have to pay for the lesson if you cancel anyway, so you go, hoping you'll get a little bit out of it even if you're not feeling prime."

"Oh, that makes sense."

I smile because, unfortunately, for many of us, it does.

My daughter is continuing with her plans for the week: "And tomorrow we're going to Laguna Beach and on Thursday we're going back to Rodeo Drive."

I sit my soup can down on the counter so I can savor the creamy smoothness later, the highlight of my day, and realize even if I never get to see her adventures via her Facebook photos, I'll still have memories, courtesy of my Chase credit card receipts.

Coloring Between the Lines

It should not come as any surprise that I discovered a large silver spike sprouting from my center hairline this week. Although some may have embraced the Unicornian symbolism, I quickly plucked it and called for an appointment with Sheila, my colorist. She squeezed me in her tight Saturday book, neglecting to tell me that it was the first of eight Prom days. So there I sat, the only person in the shop who was alive when the Beatles came to America the first time. The only person in the shop who wore bell bottoms on their maiden voyage in the fashion world. The only person in the shop who ate at McDonalds before it had inside seating.

Most people would probably have been a bit daunted by being in the center of the up-dos, sprayed curls, and easy bake tans. But, as one who has endured skating drama and competitions for years, I sat there, front and center, in the midst of those star-gazers with my head plastered in what looked like Bill Cosby Milk Chocolate Jell-O for thirty-five minutes, reading the latest issue of Cosmo with a smile on my face. As an added bonus, I now know What Really Turns Him On and The 10 Things Women Don't Even Tell Their BFFs.

Skating moms have to be tough. We face our toughest

gauntlets in the form of our offspring.

For example, my daughter has started to give me fashion tips. This is probably because she is almost twenty and would probably look great in bib overalls and a flea market t-shirt. (We will, however, never be able to confirm this, since she seems to have an allergic reaction to anything that does not have a "Must Be Dry-Cleaned" label and, like car warranties, is only used by the original owner).

She becomes the Stella McCartney to my Ellen DeGeneres wardrobe. This isn't so bad when it is done in person. It is a bit hard to take over the phone.

"Why are you getting your hair cut, you need to let it grow"?

"I'm just getting a trim and a little color."

"You always say that but then you get an inch cut off and your hair never grows. You just need to let it grow a bit more so it doesn't stop at your chin. That isn't your best look."

"Oh," I continue, mollified that I have the potential of having a good look, "I'm just happy that it is finally 80 degrees and I can wear sandals."

"What are you wearing?" She asks inquisitively.

I know, I know. Many women have written stories about having those same four words whispered into the phone. In fact, *Cosmo* had an article about the adventures of phone sex I had just started when the timer went off. Trust me, the few times anyone has ever asked me what I was wearing over the phone were asexual and more in line with whether or not I had a raincoat handy to run to the shed to check the quantity of gas in the lawn mower can.

So, I naively plunged in where no woman should go.

"I have on my Treks, my college ethics t-shirt, and my athletic pants." I knew immediately I should have reversed the order.

"You mean your sweat pants."

"Well, I think the modern term is 'Athletic Wear.'"

"The gray ones? The capris?"

"Yes!"

"Why would you wear those to get your hair done?"

I hesitate, feeling a little Robert Frostish. A road divides into the wood and I am about to take the one less traveled by ...

"They are comfortable. I am going to have work done on my body."

"You shouldn't go to any salon looking like you have low expectations. You should dress up more. What accessories can you wear with sweat pants? And if they have a draw string they are sweat pants. If you don't look like you care, they won't care."

For a moment, I am stunned. This has the echoes of things I have told my daughter in the past, mutated a bit, but formatted in some earlier words of advice for competitions.

"Even if you mess up, fall ten times, forget twenty seconds of your program, you have to keep a real smile on your face and look confident as if that was what you intended to do."

I suddenly feel a bit light-headed and dizzy, as I often feel when I realize I missed one of those major "Hints from Heloise" that everyone else seems to have mastered. This one seems to fall into the same category as the one where my friends clean their houses a bit before the cleaning service comes so they won't think they are slobs.

"I guess that makes sense," I reply slowly.

"Exactly. Why don't you put on a pair of Ann Taylor pants, but don't wear that striped top; it cuts you off too much. You need to wear something that elongates your torso."

I frown at my vintage t-shirt image in the mirror. I realize to pull this off I will now have to take the butterfly clip from my tresses and wash my hair and style it before I go to the salon.

I sigh into the phone.

"I'm going to a Seder tonight—what do you think I should wear?"

There is a long pause, and I ask the classic Verizon line.

"Yes, I can hear you. I just can't think of anything. You're going to have to go buy something."

"I have plenty of things that look like they've been to the desert."

"Exactly. Trust me on this, they won't work. You need a casual yet elegant look. Look for something by Elle Moss, but make sure it doesn't look too young. Call me from the store and send a picture ."

No problem. Before I even get to the salon I have lathered and blow-dried my old hair to make way for the new. I have read the instructions for my camera phone for the first time, and I have left my comfy clothes refolded in the dresser drawer.

A gaggle of young prom girls is nothing compared to my next hurdle.

Sometime today my daughter is going to ask what shoes I will be wearing. All those young bunioned skating feet that should be seeking comfort and cushioning? Well, they have no use for Clarks and Born.

It's going to be a long day.

Coat Closet

I have just returned home after living for 36 hours in the same clothes and the same dab of 18-hour deodorant, and we all know that not many things in the new-current era have a double-shelf life. Oh, let's be frank. I've done this a few times in my adult life, but I can count them on half of my fingers that are into the 16th day of a two-week manicure.

One time I was the sixty-first person in line to buy Bon Jovi tickets. Another rare occasion had me on the trail of an elusive Cabbage Patch doll. Still another memorable outing of wearing a t-shirt long past its ripeness occurred when the airline lost our luggage on a trek to California, and we had allotted our first day – our only free day – to explore the wonders of Rodeo Drive. We were not buzzed into any of the special boutiques that dot that coveted Beverly Hills Boulevard.

The few other times, much earlier in my life, had to do with things like Pink Squirrels and Singapore Slings which I thankfully don't remember in great detail.

So you might be disappointed to hear that I wasn't in line for tickets for Clay Aiken's new summer tour or driving cross-country as a COI groupie on this occasion.

I was helping my daughter move to her new apartment.

My daughter wanted to move closer to the rink, so we moved her from her third-floor studio apartment to a first-floor one-bedroom apartment.

Sherry Bosley | 167

In the same building.

See. You're thinking it, too: a piece of cake. It's all downhill walking basically, with more room to maneuver. It was a warm spring day; it would take a few hours tops.

Several flies fell into this ointment, and I will list them in the order of hindrance.

1. Rain
2. A two-skater birthday extravaganza the night before
3. 67 jackets
4. A cable company that uses the tin can and string method of communication.

Okay. First of all, "April showers" is a sweet vignette attached to most calendars with a photo of a little girl with a pink watering can. Yesterday was more in line with a deleted scene from "The Perfect Storm," deleted because it was raining so hard that the audience couldn't see the action. This delayed the start time considerably.

The birthday party sounded like it was successful, although I got very little information from the group of merry skating souls who arrived to help with the move. I think I heard them mention there was some "pong" playing, so my faith is restored that kids today can still find joy in some of our old classic games. I'm not sure where they found paddles in this day and age, however. Regardless, they worked hard, even if a bit slow, and they avoided loud noises like the ticking kitchen clock. My daughter also missed the cell call that the cable company made, a necessity before actually driving to the location.

My daughter's new apartment has two closets: a bedroom closet and a coat closet. The problem occurred when we realized my skating pixie has 67 jackets and coats. This must be combined with the fact that she is also is a bit of a neatnik. Yes, she color codes her clothes and subcategorizes by season and purpose, a daunting filing system for the rest of us mere mortals.

While my daughter remained in the third-floor nonpenthouse packing away, we debated how to hang the jackets in their new home.

"We could hang them by color!" offered one 20-something male.

"But most of them are black!" piped in another masculine voice.

"Let's just hang all the skating ones on the left and all the others on the right."

"I think she wears all of these to skate in."

The guys looked at each other and shook their heads. "I grew up in Alaska, and I only have three coats."

The girls took over the task and told their male counterparts to "toughen up," and "I think she has more at home than this. This must be her basic collection." While we sorted North Face and Gortex, the time slipped into evening.

The cable company provided the denouement of my adventure in extended wear. They had issued a service window of time that they failed to either write down or communicate on a modern piece of equipment. (They seemed to only use smoke signals or carrier pigeon, as no service technician arrived at any of the four quoted times. At 10:30 p.m., a supervisor advised me, after some heated discussion on my part, that she would have an able-bodied person at the apartment the following day between 10 and 2. Luck, being what it is, this time slot matched perfectly with the hours my daughter was taking some young men through their dance tests at the now, much closer rink.

So, as the mom, I offered to spend the night sans a change of clothes to be available for the service call. My daughter kindly offered to lend me some of her "larger" things. Of course, larger to her means someone gave her a size "small" instead of "extra small."

"But mom, some are really big, I think you can wear them to sleep in at least." To prove this she produced a "Green Turtle" t-shirt that was marked "S" and did appear to be pushing a size 4.

I smiled tenderly. "Sweetheart, if I try to put this on, it's going to be a remake of 'The Incredible Hulk. I'll be okay."

This morning I had the option of showering and putting on the same dirty clothes — all the dirty clothes — or just acting like I was buying Rolling Stones tickets. As I sat on the couch pondering the decision, I noticed that one of my socks was on inside out. By switching it around, I felt a tiny bit better, perhaps Feng-shuing my body.

The cable representative arrived at ten minutes before 2. In annoyance, I made sure I stood right near the personal space line while he worked.

"We're going to have to run the line through this closet," he advised as he opened the double doors and beheld the bevy of jackets and coats.

"Geez, how many people live here?"

"One."

He started moving some of the skating jackets to the sofa, noticing the various clubs and team emblems. I could see him doing a mental size chart as he nodded to me.

"My dad still has all of his old baseball team uniforms hanging in his closet too."

"Really?" I query as I slid the twenty dollar I had earmarked for a tip from my pocket back into my wallet.

"Well, that's our generation for you. We're all about having lots of clean clothes, whether we wear them or not. And, we sell a lot of channels whether you watch them or not."

Writing the Wrongs

Let me be honest. This has not been my best weekend.

For the past three years I have been working towards getting an administrative position in the field of education. This is probably the closet thing to being an indentured servant as we have in our society today. It means six or seven graduate level classes past the master's level, numerous committees, several chair positions, projects, team leadership to the third power, and leaping through several fiery hoops in a single bound. And all of this after working a full day. On Saturday I got a letter saying, "No Thanks" for this year. There is no room at the inn because no one is leaving. In skating language, this is like being the 5th or 6th place team at Sectionals. You get to fill out the forms just in case, but there is little chance there will be a call up to Nationals. A little recognition and a lot of heartbreak at being so close to getting an invitation.

So, I was feeling a little weepy and sat sipping sangría and scanning the radio for either some Carpenters or Captain and Tennille songs to sing a duet with, when my daughter called me on her way to a Kanye West concert.

"That's great," she proclaimed.

"Great? I said I *didn't* get the job."

"I know what you said, that's why it's great."

"Really? Great? You realize this may mean you have to wear the same black patent pumps for another season, right?"

"Don't be silly! You always told us that all you have to do is choose. You either work doing something you love, or you work at something that you at least like, which allows you to make enough money to let you do what you love."

I sigh. Surely, if I knew how to do needlepoint I would have made a pillow for the couch with that ditty. I am not in an Erma Bombeck mood, however.

"Mom. You love to write. You haven't been able to write because you have been too busy preparing for this job. And, if you got that job, it would have been worse. You would never have had the time. And, you know what you promised!"

Ah, yes, door number 3, when one and two were a goat and donkey. This should be the new car, but it might just be a team of mules and a herd of goats.

Although I have had several stories and essays published, I had promised to write my first book if I didn't get the job. Or finish my already started first book. Or start a second book instead of my unfinished first book.

"So now you can take the whole summer and write. You can even take your laptop to Lake Placid to edit if you have to."

"Lake Placid is 10 weeks away. I don't think I'll be finished by then. I'm not even sure what to write…"

"What are you thinking of?"

"The book I started is a bit Janet Evanovich-like. The main character is an English professor at the community college, but she used to be police officer, and she keeps getting dragged back into the criminal investigation world by her students."

"That sounds like your life."

"No, this would be fiction"

"What else?"

"I was going to write a nonfiction piece about a case I worked where a woman drugged her husband, shot him three times, and then cut his body up in eight pieces so she could carry it away in bags to bury in difference places."

"That's so gross; people wouldn't sleep at night."

"And then I was thinking of doing a novel about skating. I

have a tentative working title: "Prick of the Ice."

"Oh, that's clever; it brings in toe-picks"

" I guess you could go with that, but I was thinking more of a fiction piece about some of the public personas versus the real personalities. You know, you would have to imagine someone with a big head and a little heart. You could probably do a lot with that theme line."

"I'm not sure there would be a market for that. Maybe you should ask some other people what they think you should write. Can't you just do your weekly column as a book and make it longer. Oh, and change the skating character? Make it a boy, a skating son?"

"We'll see. Where are your tickets for the concert? Did you get lawn seats?"

"Oh you are funny tonight. Getting lawn seats would be like taking food into a restaurant; it would be rude. Besides, you always say, it's not worth going if you're more than 10 rows back."

Gosh, I talk a lot. When did she start remembering all of this?

Traveling Band

This has not been my best week. I am slowly coming to terms with things, but the transition is not all that smooth.

Oh, there were minor things. I had to endure: Jason Castro attempting to sing two Neil Diamond songs on American Idol. This, I imagine, was the equivalent of me trying to sing "Get Rich or Die Trying" by 50 Cent. I, of course, know I can't sing and would not attempt it, but some don't have my keen insight into these matters. I waited ten long weeks to hear my childhood heart throb be honored on Idol only to have it parodied by dreadlocks.

The weather knocked on my headache door all week, and once the door opened, it let in the highest pollen count in decades. I am feeling like a bee with so much dust on me that I could pollinate a rose garden by merely shaking my hair. I am now a Claritin D redi-tab junkie.

I decided to help my mood in this topsy-turvy time by eliminating the use of any past-tense verbiage by the 12th graders I teach. It's one of the perks of actually being the language police. So we lived in the "literary present" all week.

No one "stopped" anything.

Nothing "ended."

"How can we keep talking about everything in the present tense. That doesn't make any sense," they grumble and whisper with undercurrents of "hormone therapy" and shock treatments. I merely peered at them above my half-rim glasses as I walked down each aisle with a toss of my English-teacher-issue teal and purple shawl, ignoring their whines and rants.

"Let's get back to the intricacies of Canterbury Tales, shall we."

Of course the big thing is my daughter. She has this odd sense of humor. I'm not really sure where she gets it. She called me on Wednesday and said, excitedly, "Guess who is going to be sleeping in my bed?"

This is not something on which a mother wants to speculate.

I went through the visual manifestations of a Tourette's victim before I could muster a willowy, "Who?"

She laughed then, and told me the Orlando Bloom of the skating world would be using her apartment for the week she is away, as he needs a place to stay.

And of course, that is the rub.

My daughter is having the time of her life while I am wearing basic black everyday and listening to old country music songs and writing bad poetry on the backs of M & T bank receipts (a new genre I am creating). She just returned from Denver and the Governing Council meeting where she got to hear Michelle Kwan give an articulate and memorable speech, and she got to vote on issues that are "paramount to the future of figure skating." My daughter is now, or perhaps she has always been, an activist for USFSA.

She returned home for the day to repack her suitcase with five bathing suits, a few sundresses, and shorts to leave tomorrow to go to Cabo for the week. Sun, sand, and relaxation at some fabulous resort where they have pool bars manned by handsome young bartenders named Antonio or Cortez.

I, on the other hand, might get Applebee's curbside-to-go one night this week. The waitress's name is Renee and she seems to be about seven months pregnant. Although she has looked the same for about a year, I still feel compelled to give her a 30 percent tip.

I have heard that mothers are often jealous of their daughters, but I never realized until now why.

"How have you been sleeping?" I ask my peppy daughter.

"Great. I sometimes don't even remember turning off the light and putting my head on the pillow."

"That's wonderful." I smile faintly as I look at her face. Is it possible to get rosier cheeks at her age?

"Maybe you should try meditation, Mom, if you are having trouble sleeping," she offers serenely.

"Hmpph! Meditation is just thinking. I'm pretty sure I'm doing enough of that."

"Maybe you should listen to music before you fall asleep then. I'll download some songs for you on my old iPod. I think you can even get American Idol songs each week, and I know you like that."

I smile. "That would be great, sweetheart."

And there you have it. I wonder if she would understand me better if I told her about buying three single tickets to one Neil Diamond concert so I could decide which seat was the best. Those are moments you can't download on iTunes or watch on MTV. They are to quote a famous credit card ad, "Priceless."

Swapping Stories

Today I found out I have a great deal of respect for Britney Spears' father.

Oh, not because he raised two teen idols, no, no, but because he has actually made a legal stand telling the world and his daughter that "he knows best" and is taking over who makes the decisions in her life.

Oh, what a dream. Even if for only one day.

I know that for many of you this is hard to understand. You are still invited into the bedrooms to help with hair, make-up, and settle pre-event nerves, those that come with dances, first dates, a night out with friends. Those of you with daughters who are fifteen and under still probably get to pick the colors for the dance and at least make a suggestion of the cut and the line of the frock in question.

But just remember, something happens when they start driving.

It happens faster when they start driving their own cars that you pay for.

These tiny dancers start thinking they have the right to make their own decisions about everything. As they inch toward the end of their teen years, they start forgetting to even mention some of the choices they encounter along the way.

Sometimes, I admit it, I feel like Mr. Spears.

"I saw that Desmond Tutu is coming to your college in

April, are you going to go and see him?"

"I don't know, I have heard of him, what band was he with again? I don't really have any plans until Cinco de Mayo."

"When is Cinco de Mayo?"

"Are you joking me? You don't know when Cinco de Mayo is? It's in the name — Cinco — five, May — Mayo? I can't believe you don't know that?"

"Sorry, I'm a student of the seventies; we took German in high school because the threat of Big Red was hard to die."

My daughter breathes deeply into the phone, I try to flip my hair a little in a daughter-like imitation but semi-wrench my neck in the process just as she continues.

"You're not making any sense. You always have to be so symbolic."

"Sorry. Well, you should really try to catch Tutu if you can, he was an old rocker from way back with a band called 'Three Dog Night.' Make sure you tell your friends."

I laugh silently as I rub my neck. Maybe she has been too isolated in skating world. Certainly they have learned to get past World War II in high school now, although our history classes never did.

"Oh," she continues, "I forgot, I am going to a swap meet next Friday."

My blood chills for a moment, again, much as I imagine Mr. Spears felt when Britney announced her engagement to Kevin Federline, or perhaps the first time he opened a magazine and saw a photo of his daughter with the little black X indicating she had gone out sans panties.

I try to wrap my mind around the image of my daughter at a swap meet. Black leather, Harley motorcycles, du-rags on long knotted hair. Boots with round heels and steel toes.

I shake my head and wrench my neck a second time. I just can't see her on the back of a hog wearing her new silver Tory Burch quilted flats.

"Sweetheart, I don't think that's safe."

"What are you talking about, we're going to be at Gina's

apartment. Would could happen?"

I close my eyes for a moment and then say, "Okay, what are you talking about?"

"Well, a bunch of us are going to bring all of our clothes and accessories that we don't wear much anymore and throw them into the middle of the room and then we'll just sort through and pick out new things we like."

I imagine all the Abercrombie, Lacoste, J. Crew, and Ralph Lauren shirts heaped in a leaf pile on top of a coffee table, a Citizen for Humanity jean leg here, a Kate Spade belt there.

I mentally add up all the ghosts of purchases past.

"You know, sweetheart, some people have been able to recoup a bit of their money selling vintage clothing on eBay."

"Mom! What fun would that be?"

Oh — fun, right.

Oh, Baby, Baby.

Latin program exhibition piece

Falling For It

So for the second time in the last two years, Miss USA has tripped and fallen at the Miss Universe pageant. I mention this because Matt Lauer informed me of this monumental fact this morning on the Today Show.

My heart goes out to Crystal Stewart's mother.

The parent of any skater understands the significance of this blip.

We live in fear of "the fall."

We become superstitious about it. We bring our "lucky" bits of personal flotsam to ward off slipped edges and caught toe-picks. We learn to hold our breath and increase our lung capacity as the program length moves from two to seemingly 84 minutes.

During the last few competitions, I have watched the parents in the audience and am amazed at the varied degrees of watch-ability.

Some parents sit calmly; a few even sip coffee during the twizzles. Some sit on the edge of their seats with clenched hands, as if they were going through each jump and spin with their team. Some secretly gulp a few swallows from silver flasks.

I am a little suspect of the parents who can watch calmly with a sweet smile of their face. These are the same people who say things like, "Oh, I don't mind what birthday is approaching, I'll be just as happy at 70 as I am at 30." And "No, you eat the last piece of cheesecake," or "You go ahead with your full grocery cart, I have plenty of time."

I am suspect because I have also sat like that, but it was with the aid of whatever tranquilizer one of my friends brought to the rink. Seriously, I who in real life hesitates to take even a Tylenol, open my mouth for whatever my RX-savy friends choose to pop in.

It wasn't always like that. I used to feel a bit stronger than the parents who had to wait in the lobby or on the outer concourse of the arena. But, I secretly envied them, and as my daughter got in the opening pose I longed to make a run for it myself. I devised ways to watch by not watching. I would cheer and clap for them as they entered the ice, and then, when their music started, I would close my eyes. I would then listen to the music and play in my head what they should be doing — and trust me, they had all level fours in my version — while asking my friend and partner's mom repeatedly, "How is it, How is it?" (She is in banking and therefore steady as a rock. She can run a spreadsheet at the end of each program and know the variables to compare to previous performances.) I would open my eyes during parts of the program, inching out to the edge of the cliff so to speak, squinting just a little, allowing my eyelashes to shield any potential for disaster.

This descent from pseudo-watching to being tranquilized did not occur naturally.

No. It happened after I witnessed a two-fall event. That's right. I have heard the gasps two times in the same program and opened my tangled eyelashes to a double splat-fest.

The lowered scores aren't the worst part of the falls. The worst part is coming up with what to say to your offspring when they finally make their way to the stands.

Nothing works, of course. (You can discard these as tried but not successful: "That didn't go as planned"; "I wish you could skate that again"; "Well, except for about eight seconds that was a great program.")

The side affect is that once your child falls, you, as a parent, fear the reoccurrence.

This morning, Matt Lauer confirmed that fear. I didn't watch the Miss Universe pageant (although it is a great event to get costume ideas) but now I know the fallee's name and propensity of the USA candidate to fall on the steps. Matt called Crystal this morning and asked her what happened, and she was forced to come up with an answer.

But sometimes there just isn't an answer. It just happens, and we've seen it chip away at dreams big and small.

So, as the skating season nears (two weeks and counting), I might recommend the Jimmy Buffet/Alan Jackson approach to watching: It's Five O'Clock Somewhere.

Maybe sponsors should stop trying to sell their product and go with a logo on a small silver flask.

Mousey Disposition

I came to spend the night with Pilar to have a little quality time before the demands of school and the demands of the skating season come front and center.

So I can explain why I am up at 4:00 a.m.

It is true that it is difficult to sleep in a full-size bed with a person who is used to sleeping alone, especially when that person throws her firmly toned arm across your face in the middle of the night reminding you of many things, including the fact that you didn't spend those hours in the gym over the summer liked you had planned.

But what kept me hovering at the edge of sleep was the ticking of that $5.00 yard sale clock and the scurrying sounds of The Mouse. The Mouse is not a pet that was brought to the apartment by either of the girls sharing the two bedroom walk-up. My daughter comes from the typical cat-dog background, and Clare has a feline companion at her other home. (Neither girl, mind you, has ever pooper-scooped a yard or sifted through a litter box.) No, this fuzzy minute dynamo is living under the stove without the added $30.00 per month security deposit.

His presence will not generate the same feelings that Michael Jackson had when he penned "Ben."

The girls don't want to buy this one a toy convertible per Stuart Little.

Okay. It's not that we are anti-traditional pet people. When I was younger, I wanted to have a pet lion or tiger of my own, and could not understand my parents being reluctant to get the necessary permits. Good friends of mine own several snakes, turtles, lizards, and other things with scales, and I dump crickets and frozen mice into their cages when I reptile-sit for them when they go on vacation. Okay, okay, I do close my eyes as I do it and hum very loudly, so I don't overhear any crunching, but I do take care of them. (So you don't think I have weird friends, the big lizard is named RuPaul because without the wig their heads look the same. Even if you think they still might be weird, you have to admit they have a sense of humor.)

So not liking the mouse is not a prejudice against nontraditional pets. It is a prejudice against free-range rodents.

The girls want to get rid of this free-loader.

The problem is the methods for eviction are pretty straightforward. Traps or poison. We went to look at the implements of battle at the hardware store. There are basically three kinds of traps. One is baited and has a huge bar that snaps across and crushes the little mouse body. This seems so Louis XV without the blade and a bit barbaric for the current era. And, the girls were horrified to learn they would have to retrieve the body and witness the evidence of their cruelty.

The second type of trap uses some type of super glue; the mouse is lured onto the sticky pad and then cannot get free. This produced two concerns: what if they got this stuck on their own hands as they set it up, and would the mouse scream and whimper when caught. Since we would still be dealing with the body retrieval again, with this method the said body might still be alive. We passed on this method also.

The third trap seemed ideal from a practical position. The mouse is lured into a black box, the door slams shut by a hidden mechanism, and the mouse cannot escape. You pick up the box and discard it. We debated the ethical issues involved and the Edgar Allan Poeish qualities it possessed, trapping a live creature and leaving it to starve to death in a small dark prison and decided this, too, was not a method for execution. And, of course, there was the issue of who would carry the coffin with its live inhabitant to the dumpster.

I think you see the trend here.

Poison was also judged and voted inhumane, and, if used, would still leave the issue of the body needing to be relocated.

And so the skating girls live with their beady-eyed stow-a-way.

My insomnia was inspired by my thoughts at 4:00 a.m. Why would a mouse choose to live in an apartment surviving on Luna bar crumbs? Surely he smelled the brownies that were baked in 4B. A mouse that chooses to live by licking trashed yogurt lids and granola residue is a scary creature.

At 4 a.m. the imagination can take over. A mouse that is making better life choices is difficult to accept in the dawn's early light, so I get up and turn on the light.

Ben II cannot stand light. Especially the unhealthy fluorescent kitchen bulb. In the morning, well, in the more traditional morning, I will call the apartment manager. I believe they have a program to relocate apartment mice, perhaps to a new gym or yoga center, and I'll make sure the girls get put on the waiting list.

In the mean time, we'll be going out to breakfast.

Photo Op

I think it is time we talk about pictures.

Not the photos from the official photographers at competitions, where we buy several hundred prints of our sporting kids for the price of plane fare to Hawaii. No, I mean the photos we offer to the world everyday. The ones on our official documents, the ones that are requested by food store cashiers, doctor's office receptionists, and the notary public at the bank. That's right, our driver's license photographs.

First of all, it clearly states that a driver's license is to be used only for identification of operating a motor vehicle. It is not supposed to be used to verify my Visa signature, get my child out school by showing I am the official guardian, or scanned by a bartender to verify I am over 21 and do not have an alcohol restriction imposed on said license.

And presenting it is always the same; I have to surgically remove it from my wallet where is seems super-glued to the clear plastic shield. I hand it to the clerk, she looks at it, she does this little blink with her eyes, and then avoids looking at me again.

Driver's license photos are so horrible for several reasons.

First of all, there are only four or five birthdays we care about ever. We care about turning 13 because we are then a teenager. We love 16 because it means you can drive (and that whole "sweet sixteen" thing that we learned is greatly overstated). We hunger for being 18, because it signals the crossover into adulthood. Turning 20 is the final escape from being deemed a teenager, and the following year is the last of the big celebrations. Being 21 means you can actually go into a club and order a legal drink.

That's it. We don't want to celebrate any other advancements in age.

The motor vehicle department has this odd way of photographing drivers. If dog years equal one for every seven of ours, they use the Beagle counting model. That's right. Every five years we get a notice that we need to go to the MVA and renew (and get re-photographed) our privilege to drive.

This is not a cause for celebration. In fact, they won't give you the old license back in case it was a good previous photo year. They will cut the little picture out and you can use it to keep a running progress of your life at five year clips.

It is kind of like a bell curve I guess.

Passport photos are other captured moments in time. Adults always look like they are about to be incarcerated. There is no way to stand against a blue sheet draped over a concrete wall in a government building and not think the next step involves getting black ink on your fingers.

These should be happy photos.

These are the pre-photos for vacations.

Or skating travel.

The pix should not look like you were just handed a bill for the entire Olympic skating team. Eyes should not look glazed, hair should not stand on end.

We need some free-lance photographers to stand on the sidelines at motor vehicle departments and the post office passport line to assure quality control or at least competitive incentives. Someone who makes sure the light is falling softly across our cheekbones. Someone who knows what a "good side" is, and knows how to tip the chin at just the right angle to hide the recent addiction to Nutter Butters.

Passport pictures stay with us for a decade. It does seem like a sentence and there is no possibility for parole.

I am currently getting travel materials together for my daughter's Team USA competitions in France and Norway, and so, of course, I have her passport in hand. There is no denying that being on the up side of the Bell Curve has advantages.

I take some comfort in seeing the numbers and the U.S. seal that flits across her face like those holograms in a Cracker Jacks box. Still, I have been with her when custom agents look at her passport, then at her, and then smile sweetly, saying, "Great picture."

I've resigned myself to accepting there will be some things I will never hear in my lifetime,

Topping the list: The salesperson at Talbots will never say. "Great picture, Mrs. Banderas."

Security Deposits

Typically there is some confusion as to when the end of the year actually occurs. There are various reasons for this.

For teachers and administrators in both private and public schools, the end of the year occurs somewhere near the start of summer. In reality, this is about 46 days after students have mentally shut down. The last few weeks are made even less tolerable by the fact that the economy has impacted the date on which air conditioning may be turned on in these cavernous tombs of wisdom, so that "sweating to the Oldies" takes on new meaning as one tries to analyze the syntax of Beowulf with perspiration upon one's brow. Likewise the cafeteria, always known for their half-star rating, tends to mix the contents of the freezer into a goulash that has pizza slices, macaroni, and meatballs congealing in a brown stew.

The end of the year for those in accounting is a real mess. Some fiscal years end on June 30, some on Halloween, for others it falls on December 31, and, for the robust, on April 15. This causes havoc for medical and dental plans and those end-of-the-year bonuses we used to hear about in the trenches.

In the sports world, the end of the year translates to be the end of the season. It can be earlier for those who don't make the finals or the play-offs. In ice-skating, the end of the season is officially the Worlds competition in March. Skaters immediately begin working on new programs and getting costumes together for the next competitive year that officially starts for the highest level in October. If they are lucky, they may be able to squeeze in one vacation week. Apparently this isn't true for those in sport's highest pay brackets. Basketball hoopsters, baseball hitters, football linemen, and golfing duffers all take a bit of time off. By "a bit of time," I mean months. This is obvious because 97 percent of these players do not live in the town or city for which they play, so they get to go home.

My daughter trains at a rink, like thousands of other skaters across the country that does not allow them to ever go home. No red slippers clicks can get them there. It is just the process; there is no down time. Going home is only for a visit.

And so, Pilar is now on starting her fourth year of living on her own. For her college selection, she theoretically drew a circle that extended a five mile radius around her training rink in Philadelphia and applied to those institutes of higher learning, not a practice endorsed by Princeton Review, but thankfully she had a plethora of colleges and universities to consider. Her end-of-the-year is when the lease on the current apartment reaches its full term. Unfortunately, there is always a lap-over period. For example, her current 18-month lease expires on October 1. This is not an ideal time, as she will be in school and it is in the middle of the competitive season (and while it is true she is not competing this year, it is no surprise that she is at the rink just as much as when she did, and she still goes to the major events). In her search for a new apartment that meets the requirements, (washer and dryer in unit, walk in closet, bathroom with a vanity that holds at least two hair appliances, a mirror not stolen from a carnival funhouse, floors that do not squeak, and mice that have been placed in the rodent relocation program), she has discovered a "fabulous find" with all the aforementioned amenities, plus a pool and health spa, but it is only available until August 15. So, there is a six-week double payment overlap in her end of the year.

People have been pointing out that we really shouldn't just be focusing on the end of the year right now. We should be looking to Nostradamus who predicted the end of everything, the end of the world actually, on December 21, 2012. I am a bit skeptical of this hypothesis, however. The great seer foretold these events in cryptic quatrains that are left to translators versed in the skills of allusion and symbolism. Nostradamus was also by trade a pharmacist, which indicates he may have inhaled a few too many fumes from whatever substance he was pounding and grinding at the moment. For anyone who has ever purchased a blank Day Runner planner, by the time you fill out the dates for that one year you are a bit lackadaisical by October, so it seems to me that in 1557, Nostradamus could have fallen to sloppy rhyming couplets and dubious allusions as he processed through 500 years of proclamations and predictions. It seems very probable that he merely said, "Winter Solstice 2012: we're done here."

Of course, if true, this is will be a grand irony. Our children will have graduated college debt-free, as we have resisted the lure of student loans. Our home and cars will be mortgage and lien free and we will actually be thinking about when and if we can retire.

Well, if we're looking for an upside, we wouldn't have to worry about Christmas bills or the lines for exchanging gifts after the holiday. Of course we would lose the security deposit on whatever apartment my daughter is living in at the time.

Terrible Threes

My mom used to say that things happen in threes. What she didn't say was that this only occurred with bad things. You never have the possibility of getting three hot fudge sundaes at one sitting or three pairs of new shoes or three anywhere-in-the-continental-U.S roundtrip airline tickets for getting bumped.

If a flood occurred in the Midwest and a tornado touched down in the South, Mom became the oracle of foreboding about what new disaster would strike for the trifecta of doom. It became so ingrained in my subconscious that I didn't even realize I was marking disasters off as they occurred, and counting. And now, I have discovered that I have passed this three-fold tally system on to my children.

Earlier in the week, Ed McMahon passed away. Although he never came to my door with a super-sized check, and I rarely stayed awake to watch his banter with Johnny Carson, I was drawn in to his candor and charm nevertheless. When the news arrived that he had succumbed to the ravages of age, I felt saddened that we had lost another great entertainer.

On Thursday, Farrah Fawcett also lost the battle with cancer. This of course set the wheels in motion. A single event can go solo, but a duo disaster is the call for the third corner of the triangle. Farrah was a famed Charlie's Angel — from the old school — and she set the cosmetology world on blunt-cut end with a hairstyle smack-down that has only been challenged in the past by Dorothy Hamill and Jennifer Anniston.

I feel a little guilty as I started to anticipate who the next victim would be. This is really because I started to hear that weird whistling sound in my mind from "A Fistful of Dollars" in which Clint Eastwood uses one of his four dramatic acting faces. (I haven't actually watched any of those Bad and Ugly movies in their entirety, but my husband considers Clint to be eligible for sainthood when he does pass to the great western in the sky. He is not able to discuss range of acting skills in an unbiased discourse.)

I knew there would be a third. It has been prophesied. What I didn't expect was (1) my son would text me with "It is so weird that things do come in threes, and (2) that he would continue with "Michael Jackson just died."

I cannot really say why I was shocked. The MJ saga had all the foreshadowing of a bad ending of some kind. Yet, most of us over the age of forty would admit (to close friends anyway) that during Michael's career highs, we have all tried to moonwalk. Some of us would even fess up to knowing and performing the entire choreography of "Thriller" and "Billie Jean" — even if it was in the privacy of our own family rooms or a dance club that will remain unnamed (one of many reasons to be relieved that cell phone cameras with video feedback were not prevalent in the 80's).

Some people would even admit to getting a bit misty–eyed when hearing the tender lyrics of "Ben" and hearing the break in a young boy's voice, all of this dedicated to pledge loyalty and love to a feral rat that came out at night to snitch some Cheetos and was cast in the role of "best friend." Perhaps nothing symbolizes Michael's innocence more than this.

So now I hope that there will be a slight twist in the "things in threes" forecast. It will be very progressive if the figure skating community abandons overused and overworked programs like "Carmen" and "Bolero" for some classic MJ classics like "Black and White," "The Way You Make Me

Feel," and "Don't Stop Til You Get Enough."

Would it bring the house down to have a Theatre on Ice team create an entire program of "Thriller" and "Billie Jean" — moonwalk skating and all?

It is regretful that so many did not get to experience Michael Jackson first hand. By the time my children were old enough to appreciate the magic, the first of the tragic court cases was front-page fodder. Michael Jackson became an allusion for comics and movie scenes. After watching "The Wedding Singer" many years ago, Pilar queried me about how and why I would have been a fan of a man who wore his pants too short and sported a silver glove.

"It's hard to explain. It is really something you have to experience in person."

I gave both kids an opportunity to see the King of Pop in person. Michael and a star-studded cast performed for the "United We Stand" concert in Washington after the tragic events of 911. If you ever want to cure your pre-teens from being concert junkies, take them to a fourteen-hour marathon with 45-minute gaps between acts for stage set-up.

But they did get the benefit of watching Michael leave the stage in the bucket of a Cherry-Picker and moonwalk across the stage.

And now that a few days have passed since his death, the headlines are changing to wills, estates, and custodies. It is a good reminder to all of us to have our own children put sticky notes of the bottoms of anything they want while we are still alive.

And of course, there will be three commercial ventures that are guaranteed to be collecting revenues from the early passing of Michael Jackson.

Today at a local Arts and Crafts festival I heard three (times 10) cell ring tones made popular by the youngest member of Jackson Five.

There is probably a Broadway musical being penned at this very moment, possibly using the working title of "ABC."

And, of course, the glove making industry is guaranteed a 100 percent profit if they market the one glove sales approach.

Spinning

It is difficult being the mother of athletes. My daughter could model for one of those "Tickets to the Gun Show" t-shirts and my son runs six miles as a warm-up to real running.

Living in a two story house, I try not to do open-mouth breathing when I take the laundry upstairs.

I believe I am their inspiration. But not in the way you think.

I think I am their mental refrigerator magnet.

You know, the ones that are supposed to turn you away before you open the door. I am sure they are convinced this could be a mutant genetic gene that might expand at any moment.

They are subtle in their attempts to get me to "tone up."

My son bought me four spin classes at the community college for Mother's Day. I took my craft bag thinking we would be making tie-dyed yarns. Imagine my shock when I discovered the room filled with women in spandex and stationary bikes.

Okay, I thought. I can do this. I have on flip-flops, but hey, I've been riding a bike since I was six, how hard can it be?

Calling this a "spin" class was as deceiving as calling a pit bull a lap dog. It sounds so gentile and relaxing, like there might be mint juleps and cucumber sandwiches waiting later in the parlor.

The ladies mounted their bikes and took off at speeds approaching that of light. At one point, I actually saw the shifting prism. If we had been connected to a power plant, we could have supplied enough electricity to keep the southern hemisphere in a 100-watt glow.

I don't recall how it actually ended. I think there may have been a paramedic, or else it was a swimmer with a white towel around his neck. The instructor called my house a few days later and told me she had never seen anything like it: that I had hung in there for seven minutes. She told me a refund was in the mail in case I was tempted to try to increase my endurance.

My daughter on the other hand advises me about hair styles. She tries to steer me away from short hair cuts.

"Short hair doesn't look good with the shape of your face."

I look in the mirror and have trouble seeing different shapes, as everything just looks like, well, a face.

"I think you need to let it grow out," she adds.

"Really. Don't you think it will look a bit, well, lanky?"

"No."

She says this a bit too firmly, like maybe I have a cowlick at the back of my head and don't know it.

"Having longer hair will make your face appear a bit longer," she elaborates. "It won't look so ... round."

Oh, I have a round face. Ah, the classic "pie hole."

"Maybe I should just tease my bangs."

"No. You actually should get rid of the bangs, feather them into the sides."

My daughter has become Jose Eber.

She is the Joan and Melissa Rivers on the hair runway of life.

"How about a headband?"

She looks at me. "Are you six?"

Maybe I'll get a perm, I think. But I keep it to myself. Better to surprise her from my seat in the stands at her next competition.

Common Scents

So here is the problem with being a mom and being the mom of a child who is involved in a sport: We never feel we have done everything we can.

It is worry times two.

It is fretting to the second power.

The older the child gets, the less you feel able to do as a mom.

In my case, I have found the best coaches, the best training facility, the best choreography, the best costumes, the best music — or at least, that was the intention.

Life is about compromise, however, and sometimes you have to make adjustments for what is possible and what isn't possible. Sometimes there is just no more bend in the Gumby stick of life.

For example, I could have been Mrs. Jimmy Buffett, but I have an aversion to tequila. Some hurdles are just too high to get over. No one can "Waste Away in Diet Coke with Lemonville."

So you sit and do the check-off list of everything that should be done, has been done, will be done, and there is always this void that feels a bit like maybe you left the iron on when you went out. There is always the question of what "else" can I do to "help."

Today I found a new source of enrichment.

This is not easy to talk about, because I don't know the proper name for all of the entities involved in this process.

I have already mentioned how much my daughter and I "symbolically" hold on to good luck tokens. Even if we didn't quite believe, we certainly wouldn't bring on a storm of bad karma by not at least respecting the possibility.

That is the preface for explaining that today I went to see a good "witch" or a casual reference for a person who "knows rituals to perform."

This was not easy.

These people are not listed in the phone book, nor did I get a coupon in my Valu-pack mailer.

No, I overheard a conversation at a dinner party last year, and I filed it away in my memory schema of "things I might need in the future."

I can sense your skepticism here.

I feel a little of a "this woman is losing it" vibe. (I guess from this experience I have developed a bit more of the psychic power all moms possess.)

Some would say, uh-oh, this is just another way to get in on the constant cash flow pushed on parents.

Wrong!

Because this woman doesn't charge anything, nor does she accept donations.

I know. It is hard to believe. Even the waitress at a buffet restaurant expects 15 percent for bringing drinks and a stack of plates.

I went to this good luck guru's place of business (at the local community college where she is a professor). I know, you were thinking Sandra Bullock and Nicole Kidman, and a little shop that sells lotions and soaps.

She told me *exactly* what to do to bring good luck and support when my daughter skates in future competitions.

I have to burn two candles. (I can't tell you the color because they need to be specific to your own needs.) I have to look intently into the flames and "make my request known." I must write an identified number on a piece of paper, sprinkle cinnamon on it, fold the paper, and keep it with me all day. Close to my heart.

Okay, so I am feeling a little bit better. I now have a plan of action instead of just sitting in the stands and sending a mental email to all deities and muses for help when I see her guards come off before she steps on the ice.

Of course, now I can be easily identified.

I will be the mom in the stands whose Marshalls/T. J. Maxx bra smells like French toast.

Gifts that Keep on Giving

With the holiday season just around the corner, I thought we might want to go over the gift list again. Oh, not for the kids.

You know how the offspring always ask you, "What would you like this year, Mom?"

And we always answer, "Oh, nothing. I already have everything I could possibly want. I just enjoy watching you open your presents."

This year I think we should do some inner reflection and give them something solid to put in our stockings.

So I've made a list, which you can hand out to the kids. As you can tell, most of these are without cost, since gifts with cost are merely an added expense to – well – us.

But remember, the thought makes them priceless.

Top Ten List of Presents That Kids Can Give Their Parents.

1. A "Top 8" spot on your MySpace or Facebook account. Even if we do not have an account, the symbolism would be appreciated. I know there is much jockeying for position, so I

would not expect a 1 to 4 ranking. But please, even Tom is on 64 percent of teen MySpace accounts, so why not Mom?

2. A "thank you" card that you have prepared in advance, to be handed out during the year for exceptional parenting. This might be for something like a seven-hour trek in the rain to watch SkateAmerica; giving you the suede boots before Christmas, because they would look so cute with your jeans; or just for the extra fifty bucks, so you don't have to eat vanilla yogurt without fruit for the entire week.

3. A request for a photo of the two of us. I know, I know, these are not as good as the 963 photos that you self-shot at arms length of yourself with friends, but the gesture would be appreciated.

4. A photo you allowed to be taken during the year, when you actually did not complain or roll your eyes or sigh like you were taking a breathing analysis test. After this photo, you would continue to smile and ask, "Was that good, would you like to take another one just to be sure?"

5. A coupon for a dinner with us, the parents. This would be used at our discretion and would involve dining, dinner conversation, and never looking at your watch to see how much longer you think you will have to sit there.

6. Breakfast at home, at the table, with everyone sitting down at one time. No one would have on pajamas and nothing with a Kellogg's label would be on or near the table. Whatever was on the table would have pure vanilla as an ingredient.

7. A night at the movies, in a real theater for a just-released, long awaited film. And one other thing: not a matinee. You might be seen out with me in the night hours. Afterwards we could go to Coldstone and try a new ice cream creation. This is best offered in the winter.

8. A snow day. Actual snow optional. This is a pajamas-on-the-couch-with-blankets morning, watching old movies like "Dirty Dancing" or something the Olsens were in when they were under 15 or one of the Mutant Ninja Turtle movies.

9. A book discussion. This is really an extended gift: I get

you a book you asked for sometime during the year, one that you have been dying to read, and then you are so enthused about the plot and character development you ask me to read it too. I do, and then we have this long discussion on the common threads the theme weaves through the book, and the implications they have on the social connections in our real world.

10. And the Number One Gift we could ask our kids to give us – this is where you can make it personal – so for me it's this: if I suggest a song for you to skate to, don't act like I tried to pair up 50 Cent and Charlotte Church. At least mull it over, consider making it an exhibition piece to be skated at the local rink if nothing else.

Remember, sneering and ridicule have no place amongst the mistletoe.

Treating for Tricks

It is hard to think of Halloween as a real holiday, but it is my daughter's favorite. Actually the candy industry sells $3 billion worth of sugary treats during the last weeks of October, with M&Ms hoarding the most revenue with a whopping $75 million in those little candy shapes that melt in your mouth and not in your hands.

I buy bags of candy every week as I grocery shop, but oddly enough, it is never around to hand out to the little ghosts and goblins that come to our house on the last day of the month, and I am scrambling the day before to make an educated guess of how much more candy to buy for the big hand-out night. This time I don't buy candy that anyone in my house likes — this is strictly Dum Dums and Hot Tamales time.

This year will be especially hard for me. With Pilar living in skater's paradise in the urban Philadelphia Mecca, and my son "beyond all that," I am left at home to secretly miss the ghosts of Halloweens past.

Maybe some of you are missing the orange and black madness as much as I am, because it seems like all ice dancers are Halloween buffs.

How else can you explain the love of dressing up in sequins and spandex and wearing elaborate make-up?

If you want to see the evolution of society in our country, go back and look at the Halloween costumes that your kids have worn through the years. Most babies start off as either a pumpkin or a bunny or bear. This evolves into whatever Disney princess is fashionable or whatever action figure has been promoted by Saturday morning cartoons.

We have a virtual "Stars on Ice" wardrobe at home, with Jasmine, Mulan, Mermaids, and Sleeping Beauty. Of course we have coordinating costumes of Aladdin, Mufasa, the Red Power Ranger, Barney and Baby Bop, and an Orange M&M (not sure if the candy company got a piece of that purchase).

On our best costume year, my daughter wore a skating competition dress and old skates and went as Michelle Kwan/Tara Lapinski, Olympian skater. It cost us nothing extra, but seemed a bit over the top as far as Halloween costumes go. I mean, what other eight-year-old wore a $500 dress?

Even thought she is no longer a child, I tried to help my daughter come up with a costume idea this year. Please note, she did not ask me to do this, but I butted in as mothers are known and expected to do. My first idea revolved around these great vintage sequined dresses in hot pink and raging red that I have collected. (This is a long story, and we better not get distracted with that now.) These dresses could go into Motown, Vegas, or a showgirl theme, but they were given the thumbs down. Without much consideration, I might add.

My daughter said she wanted to be a "flight attendant," so I looked online for a possible source of costume selections for her.

And I was shocked.

What flight school did these attendants graduate from?

I have never been served or assisted in the air by anyone wearing a four-inch skirt and jacket with cut-outs.

It thought perhaps I had gone to the wrong website, so I clicked out and went to another site that offered fire and police costumes.

Okay, I'm pretty sure that most police officers don't carry handcuffs with fur on them.

When did Halloween costumes become so sexy?

Where are the pumpkins and ghosts?

How are kids supposed to go from being Dorothy from the Wizard of Oz to Sheena, sex goddess of the jungle when they turn 18?

My daughter told me she was making a costume, so I decided not to ask her what it was going to be, as I may never be able to fly United again and am afraid of destroying more stereotypes.

Since I was feeling a little blue, without the future hope of wandering the sidewalks with a flashlight and filled candy sacks, trailing squealing children yelling, "Trick or Treat," I went to my hair stylist for a body wave.

As I sat in the chair under those harsh lights, I felt the irony of Halloween upon me after all.

"Don't you just love those curls?" my hairdresser asked.

Great, I thought. Now I look just like Howard Stern for the holiday season. Hopefully no one will say, "Great costume."

Coming Out of the Closet

The hard thing about being on a diet is that you are "on" it. This implies you can at some point get "off" a diet. But, in reality, this is not at all like being "on" an escalator, or being "on" an airplane. The truth is, this becomes a way of life. If you get off, it has the same outcome as getting off a 737 before it lands. Lets just say, "You plummet."

I have spent my adult life surrounded by people trying to lose weight. Women typically diet, while men "cut back."

In my own house, I am sandwiched by children who are physically active and who make healthy eating choices. My son runs seven miles for fun. I hesitate to drive seven miles without a purpose, like going to the Dairy Queen or the Macy's one-day sale.

My daughter eats organic produce and leans toward the taste buds of a vegetarian. The sight of mayonnaise sends her into a shuddering spasm, even when paired with a nutritious main course like banana and white bread.

My husband is tall and lean. This is ironic because he eats two helpings of each entrée and never gains an ounce. At night he 'cuts back' from his usual three scoops of ice cream by having a bowl of cereal and one plop of ice cream in the middle.

Every night. This is of course while I eat one miniscule 100 - calorie bar.

I am attempting to change my eating habits. By this, I mean I am migrating away from finding joy in food. I am attempting to view and use food as a "fuel" source only. This is a hard concept to wrap your mind around for several reasons. The first is that some foods taste better than others. Any combination of chocolate, peanut butter, and cake hits a ten on my food-o-meter. The substitute of sugar-free gelatin does not even move the meter. The second reason changing your eating style is difficult is that we are a nation that celebrates by "dining out." A birthday, a promotion, an anniversary are all augmented by the notion that we must go to a sit-down ceremony of savory scents and tastes. We get caught up in the wine sauces, the sprig of greenery on the rim of the plate, the chocolate drizzle on the dessert tray.

It is hard to turn away from the sensory overload to the grim reality of the portion sizes of Lean Cuisine.

Since this choice wasn't a natural process, I have to admit I was directed by other factors.

My daughter, as always, is a force to be reckoned with. She, as most women, worries about gaining a pound or two. This would push her to burst from a pair of double zero jeans into a mere single digit of nothing. So she will forgo a dollop of whip cream, she will pass on the butter or cream cheese, and she will turn her head from the sight of a croissant or blueberry muffin. Although she rarely comments, when she witnesses my consumption of a slice of cake or a mound of mousse, the look on her face is as distressed as if she had just witnessed me heat a hit of gravy in a spoon and mainline it into my forearm.

My son is in pursuit of a medical career. In his spare time, he talks about "Body Mass Index" and calipers to access the percentage. He eyes me the same way others salivate over the newest Taco Bell commercial. I sleep sporadically in case he creeps into my room in the night with his instrument of mass deconstruction.

The remaining reasons have to do with my driver's license information and my closet.

We live in an era that is obsessed with identification. We have threats of terrorism and identity theft hovering over our social security and banking information. Our only proof that we are who we say we are is in the cellophane window of our wallets: our drivers licenses. This is the proof positive. Most women, however, run the risk of being called out of line, being denied access, or being asked for a subsequent form of ID, because their weight on their drivers license is not accurate. It is the one thing we don't update. Even my tiny dancer daughter is not the 101 pounds listed from her age sixteen permit. She has now added on a whopping three pounds. I, on the other hand, have added the weight circle of a large bag of dog food, the ones you struggle to balance when shifting from the cart to the car.

A woman's closet tells her life story. There is the bridesmaid dress in the back that she will never wear again but is still good for laughs. There is the little black dress from fifteen years ago when little black dresses were more about being little, maybe about having cutouts and showing more cleavage. There may even be a pair of lace-up jeans and a sweater vest.

But the real story is the range of sizes. There is the actual size, the former size, and the size she wants to be. Typically recent purchases of the last two are only for extremely great sale items.

Eventually a woman has to ask herself the hard questions:

"Do I want to update my driver's license data with the correct information or have some 23-year-old, MVA line clerk call me out on it?"

"Do I want to make some room in my closet by eliminating just one size?"

"Do I want to try on bathing suits in front of the tri-fold mirror in Macy's?"

The answer will either tip the scales against Tasty-Kakes and Ben and Jerry's or not.

Then you will be "on" an altered eating plan. And then you sit back and wait for people to notice. And they do!

"That's great mom," says my 104-pound offspring. "Now when are you going to start an exercise program to firm up everything?"

Slip-Sliding Away

When I was a young girl, there were several occasions when you went shopping to buy a new dress: Christmas, Easter, and the first day of school. Occasionally, there would be a bonus event thrown in, but regardless, the outcome was always the same: some scratchy, ill-fitting garment that required the layering of slips and tights would become the flagship for the event,

This has changed as much as Radar O'Reilly's first crank up "cell" phone has evolved into the iPhone.

For one thing, girls no longer wear slips, or petticoats as my grandmother used to hail them.

"Mom, it's the 21st Century!" my daughter proclaims as I hold a five-inch bit of lace and satin (her size) up for her inspection. "What is the point?"

"It's like a layer of insulation; it's the same thing as men wearing white t-shirts under their street clothes."

"They don't do that anymore either. Unless they want to layer colors."

"Some still do ..."

"Yeah, if they're getting AARP brochures in the mail."

I'd like to believe my daughter is a bit skewed by events in her life. She can't possibly view the world as it really is since her "big dress" dress purchase was not for the senior prom, but for her first international Junior Grand Prix event. The coveted high school letter jacket was replaced for her by the yearning and earning of the Team USA jacket.

I could think this, but then I walk into a Victoria's Secret store in the mall. Girls used to buy their underwear in packages of either three or seven. Now they buy single servings in bins that hold "boy shorts," low-rise, low-low rise, thongs, and string thongs. Briefs take on a more literal meaning in this venue. No bin is labeled "Panties."

There are also 836 types of bras. Some with padding, some without, demi-cups, full cups, half cups, cups that make you look one size larger, cups that minimize. There are displays of lingerie and sleepwear.

There is nary a slip to be found.

"We have Spanx," the salesperson answers my query and directs me to a boxed display of what my grandmother would have described as girdles in her heyday. The new prototype is flesh colored and seems to work on the same premise as a sausage casing.

What surprises me the most in shopping in this Mecca of underwear is the ratio of males to females. It is a dead heat: 50-50. The men are not there to make purchases, they are there as fashion consultants. They give a thumbs up to this bra or that, they make the final decision between the boy shorts with the pink dog logo or the low-rises with the "Pink University" imprint.

Most of this would make sense to me if camisoles had not made a comeback ten years ago. Even my grandmother told my great-grandmother, "That's sick," meaning that it would evoke projectile vomiting if forced to wear it, and not the current Lady GaGa "That's the best thing I have ever had come into my line of vision" meaning.

Camisoles now come in every color, and girls wear so many of them that their shoulders look like wound Maypoles with all the straps.

"That's different." my daughter tries to explain, "they're more about contrast than necessity. In fact, they are more of an accessory."

She stops me before I can form a line of questioning. "Besides, no one is wearing those anymore."

Pilar is sitting on the bed as I buckle the belt of a new dress I just purchased due to a recent promotion. She is looking not at the shiny surface of my half-inch belt but at my legs sheathed in Hanes "Taupe Tropic" nylons.

She is making a should-I-or-should-I-not face of indecision.

"What?" I finally cave.

"It's June." She says, as if I were creating a new Almanac.

"I know." I reply pointing to my short sleeves.

She grimaces.

"No one wears nylons in the summer anymore."

I look down at my legs and then at my toes peeping through the slingbacks.

"My legs are not tan yet, and these are sandal toes."

"Right. And those little lines across the tops of your toes are invisible."

I look down at the little worm-like seams across the ends of my toes. I remember the seams that used to run up the backs of my grandmom's legs.

"Why didn't you tell me?" I asked her as I kick off my shoes and wrangle the pantyhose off my legs.

"I don't think they send out bulletins on this, you just kind of know these things."

You either know these things or not is her implied message.

I slide my shoes back on and stand for her inspection, "Okay, how does this look?"

She closes one eye and looks at me.

"Good," she offers, "But your slip is showing."

Driving Force

I hate the part where your kids think they know more than you. Well, I mean aside from the VCR, DVR, and operational components of 20 remote controls.

My daughter has been driving for five and a half years, and my son for three. Somehow they feel this qualifies them to give information to the National Highway Safety Council.

If my daughter is forced to ride with me, it is major leg-shaking time. You know what I mean: the crossed legs, the free leg slapping time in annoyance instead of to Bobby McGhee. She, of course, selects the music or brings her own CDs, in case I might subject her to Toby Keith, Celine Dion, or the soundtrack from "Philadelphia." Her CDs are typically compilations that she self-titles "Sexy" or "Warm-up." The warm-up is her rendition of my "Sweating to the Oldies" with Richard Simmons; she apparently shares her choices with the skating session during the four or five minutes of stroking. Now I get to listen to Justin Timberlake get sultry and out of breath.

Having her as a passenger is not as pleasant as it used to be, say when she was belted into a car seat with a juice bottle in her mouth. Now, she serves as the commentator for my driving. At a traffic signal she alerts me at the speed of light and sound when the device turns green, those nanoseconds apparently add up and take time away from her that is needed for more important events, such as plucking her eyebrows or watching reruns of "Grey's Anatomy."

If we are on the interstate, she advises me that I can "get over," although I had no intention of repositioning my car. She also has the habit of leaning over and looking at my speedometer as if it is a cousin to Sleeping Beauty's mirror and will advise her who is the "Slowest in the Land."

She is also a human GPS. In her case, this means Girl Pestering System because she rarely knows where she is in actuality—I mean, she knows how to get there, unless there is a detour, or you ask her what state she is in. Then you just get the rapid blinking, no answer bit. But the real pestering comes from the apparent onset of psychic abilities that renders her capable of reading other drivers' minds.

"I think that guy behind you wants you to speed up."

"I think that car behind you wants you to get over so they can go around."

You can never use humor in these situations.

"Really. Did he have a chili cheese dog for lunch?" is just greeted with a look that questions if she will need to take over the wheel because I have become demented.

My son does not have quite the skill that my daughter has in making me think I should turn in my license. He has another technique. He just won't ride with me. He finds ways to avoid ever being a passenger. If it is required, he slumps low in the seat so positive identification is impossible. I sense his tension, however, and wonder if Jeff Gordon's mother feels the same when Mr. NASCAR drives her to a doctor's appointment.

I wouldn't mind if this sense of superior knowledge extended into other areas, say into toilet bowl cleaning or dusting. I would love for them to whip the Clorox wand out of my hand in apparent disgust and say, "It's better if you go counter clockwise first!"

But that hasn't happened yet.

I am dreading the Thanksgiving drive to the aunt's house with all the suggestions of when to change lanes, which toll booth is faster, and what the guy in the Miata thinks of how

long my turn signal has been on.
 Maybe we'll take two cars.

Pilar Bosley and Juliana Cannarozzo for Team USA at a Junior Grand Prix in Norway

It Must Have Balls

The packing for annual trek to Lake Placid for the annual Ice Dancing Championships made me realize that a kayak would have come in handy. First of all it would have looked like we were really going on vacation, and I could have stuffed quite a few items in that center hole. The weatherman projected a Bermuda High for this area that will bring the temperatures into the 100s, and the map takes it all the way to the Canadian border. (I'm not really sure how we have such a problem with border security when the National Weather Bureau can stop the weather at the border.) It is hard to imagine 95 to 100 degrees in the New York mountains.

So with departure imminent, I wanted to come clean on another issue. There is a second reason my husband does not come with me to competitions, or at least to important ones.

He has trouble recognizing skating as a sport. There should be support groups for this, but so far I have not discovered any.

To cope, we have developed this pattern or strategy, where I supply him with cursory information that does not require questions or comments, and if he feels he needs to make a statement, I reply, "That's an interesting perspective."

This is our standard operation so we can co-exist, probably much like the NFL has with John Madden fans; they get no information, but they go through the motions of listening.

Sometimes I have been lulled into believing I can still convert him, but this always ends in a Republican/Democrat 2006 type division. He totally believes the skaters are athletes; he just feels their efforts are abused because he is prejudiced against any sport that does not use a ball, is not timed, or does not have clearly defined rules that spectators can follow. Subjectivity is not something he respects; in fact, when he thinks an umpire uses it, there is a bit of posturing and calls for visits to the eye doctor.

"In golf," he says, "the ball either goes in the cup or it doesn't. There is no way a golfer can earn more points because his ball came close to the hole in an artistic manner than someone who actually sinks it."

So it is much easier for me when he doesn't come to watch.
Example.

Last September he attended a competition at our club. He innocently asked why we had three coaches on the boards for our team's event.

"Because they each have a different skill they bring to the kids," I answered.

"And how much do they charge an hour?"

This is tricky; tell the truth, but allow for misinterpretation.

"$85.00 an hour".

"Per coach?"

Cornered, you must always do the right thing.

"Did you bring the camera?" Try to change the subject.

"You're holding it. Per coach?" My husband can never be distracted about money.

"Yes. But warm-up is only five minutes."

"What can they tell them in five minutes they don't already know?"

I sigh. This is like being in a back-up on the interstate. Do you wait it out or get off at the next exit and weave your way through. Either way will be annoying.

"Well, they can tell them to keep their shoulders up, or their head up, or to go deeper in the knees."

"And they don't know that by now?"

"They all get nervous at competitions."

"Suppose I offer the kids $255.00 cash not to mess up."

I give him the look.

"Okay, but they waste a lot of time in five minutes. They skate around, fall or whatever and then go back over to the boards to talk to the coaches. It would be more cost effective if the coaches would just use a signal system."

"What are you talking about?"

"I mean, they could hold up one finger to signal, 'You messed up, do it again.' Two fingers could mean, 'Keep your back straight.' Three could …"

"Don't be ridiculous, that wouldn't work. The coaches also help boost their spirits and …"

"So get some cheerleaders over in the penalty box!"

"That's an interesting perspective." I change the subject, "I really love the costumes on the ice, the colors really pop."

"Hummf" My husband knows these are dangerous waters. "So tell me again why there are so many different costumes?"

"Because each team brings their own style to the dance!"

"But, I thought this was a compulsory dance?"

"It is."

"So they are all doing the same dance? Isn't there only one correct pattern?"

"Yes."

"Wouldn't it be easier to judge if all the teams wore the same costume, like the same black, no sequins, dress, and guys wore the same black pants and shirt?"

"The judges aren't influenced by costumes."

"So they don't get any points for the costume?"

"No, but they can get deductions if it's inappropriate or something comes off."

He is speechless for a moment as I imagine him thinking of the Mets and their matching uniforms. Time for distraction and refocus.

"Would you mind getting me a Diet Coke? I might want

dessert with dinner tonight."

You just cannot explain the nuances of skating to a bat-and-ball kind of guy.

If I Were A Man, or Beyonce's Upgrade

Two weeks ago I went to a retirement dinner for a teacher who had worked more than thirty years in public education. She was a fabulous educator and many came to offer accolades and testimonials. Through the roasting and the toasting, her family sat at the front table until it was their turn to speak. Both daughters came to the microphone and elaborated on what a role model their mother was to them, how they had grown to value the written word, how they had felt the confidence to pursue their own post graduate careers, and how they had modeled their own motherhood experiences by what they had lived. There wasn't a dry eye in the house. Everyone present realized the greatest tribute offered was from those two young women who so eloquently spoke of a passion ignited by the most important woman in their lives.

It is events like this that make one take note of her own life. There are many who feel as Frank Sinatra crooned: there are no regrets. Others wish there were do-overs.

I don't think I have any regrets on the big screen. There are moments though, in looking back, that I wish I had cataloged a bit more carefully and skillfully. There are pictures that are fading a bit around the edges in my mind that I wish I had used a Canon Sure-Shot to preserve, there are afternoons I could have waited to vacuum the rug and maybe colored another picture or two, there are those days off of school when I should have insisted we go to the museum.

I have some future regrets perhaps — which is ironic, because knowing this means I have time to correct it. But it isn't that simple.

I want to leave a few words, a phrase, a mantra, a voice of advice of sound reasoning that can be held to ward off the crushing blow of a disappointment, the bitterness of something loss, and the acknowledgement of something valued that is found, for my own children. Perhaps this is the secret desire of all parents.

But it seems all the good ones have been given.

Emerson, Gibran, Frost and a million less famous souls have found the one piece, the one antidote, the perfect quote to have emblazoned on their children's hearts and minds for eternity

I have moments when it seems to be hovering on the roof of my mouth ready to leap onto my tongue tip and fly forth from my mouth — a soliloquy of my soul left alone to dine on the fine flavors of love and maternal pursuits. Instead, something else flings itself from my mouth and it usually takes verbiage as something unorthodox or unconventional like, "Promise you will never swim in a quarry!" or "The Tin Man in the Wizard of Oz didn't have a penis."

These are things my children remember, but not for the intended reason.

The closest thing to eternal witticism that I have offered is something I said to my daughter on the topic of love.

(As a point of reference, she did not bring up the topic, and actually tried to avoid and ignore my repeated thrusts of inquiry into the matter of the heart). (I should point out as a triangulation point she was in a relationship that ended with that classic line from *How to Dump Girls 101* — "It isn't you, it's me.") (I should also point out that she still seems to hold this young man as the bar by which she measures all others, with the possible exception of Charlie White, ice-dancer extraordinaire. But he lives 900 miles away, so this cannot be put to any real test, not even an offer for coffee or conversation.) (I should also note that I myself place this young man at the very lowest bar for comparison, as he dated her for a year and then broke up with her within minutes of her birthday, and just prior to her skating in a major international competition.) (In case there is any doubt of what I clearly define as "caddish behavior," said young man did enjoy the benefits of pre-season tickets to a much-anticipated rivalry between two major NFL teams 36 hours before said *adios*, as the tickets were purchased by my daughter five months before kick-off.) (You should also note that the distance between these two points on said measuring bar due to interpretation of aforementioned actions is one we don't often call into discussion or discourse for obvious reason.) (Okay, it should be noted that, in all honesty, I did vocalize at length about Apple's subliminal influences in our social interactions by the influx of "I "products: iPhones, iTouch, iPods. This transfixes and obsesses weaker beings with, well, the "I," as in self and the "I" as in self-absorbed.)

With this required background knowledge, most would agree with me and understand, perhaps even cheer, my subsequent offering of possible insights into the complexities of male and female relationships, and perhaps even suggest a text on the issue, say even a copy of the book, *I Used To Miss Him ... But My Aim Is Improving*, by Alison James.

From this fertile ground, my best advice to date took root.

I explained to my daughter that the man she ultimately chooses to stand beside and with will have my blessing and my full support — regardless of who that turns out to be. But I wanted her to consider my most ardent desire on that road of discovery. The one wish I have for Pilar (and Adam also, although he made himself scarce when the L word came into auditory range), besides being healthy, is that she finds someone who loves her more than I do.

If she finds someone who loves her more than I do, then I am assured that the man who loves her thinks of her when he first wakes up. This is not a consequence of responsibility, or obligation, it is a life function that is as necessary as breathing and having hot coffee each morning; the thinking of her brings a wave of happiness that envelopes him to make him not a shadow that stands behind her, not a weightlifter who would try to hoist her higher, but a man who would have her hand as they run along the waves of this beach we call life. In sand and current, sometimes one leads, sometimes one lingers, but the bond is never broken.

If she finds a man who loves her more than I do then I know that she has someone who always considers her: what would make her sad, what would disappoint her, what would make her smile, what would bring a sigh of contentment, what would surprise and transfix her. A man who loves her more than I would know there is never a way to keep the darkness at bay, but he would be there with her to discover the light again, and to dance from the sheer joy of finding the one special gift that is not delivered to all, the joy of finding and knowing love.

A man who loves her more than I do would grow with her, taking nourishment from her mind and her thoughts; he would not stay in one spot of time; he would not linger in the here and now, or get lost in the what-ifs. A man who loves her more than I would help her pack for the journey, but leave room for things along the way. A man who loves her more than I would understand she needs a space to pack what she wants or needs without review, and would have the knowledge that she left room for his choices also.

A man who loves her more than I do, would say, "It's not you, it's we.

My daughter will turn twenty-one this year, so hopefully I can develop this into something of eloquence, hone the rough points until they run smooth on the mind.

My husband heard me reading this message out loud and

asked me why I didn't say, "A man who loves you more than we do." I looked at him for a moment and considered telling him the best quotes were never from Mr. and Mrs. Emerson, Mr. and Mrs. Sophocles, or Mr. and Mrs. Chinese Proverb before discarding it. He'd probably want to be avant-garde. I could have told him this is my space in the suitcase of our life, but I didn't.

"That isn't in the right syntax," I replied.

Pilar Bosley and John Corona in Turkish Original Dance program, or "Now we have Halloween costumes for life."

Acknowledgements

TOE PICK: a device that offers better purchase on the ice and the ability to stop a forward fall after a jump. But like all good things in life, it comes with the knowledge that any bump on the ice in normal pursuit can catch and send you spinning out of control or flat on your face.

I often wonder at all those verbose speeches at the award shows. When the music signals they are to relinquish the stage they are still calling names. In reflection, I now understand why the lists are so long, and just how many people are involved in the creative process.

I must offer my daughter Pilar first billing in the gratitude parade; she let me spotlight her life and exaggerate everything but her clothing size. In mirror image, my son Adam often seemed not part of the narrative, but he was always my most critical reader and spot of comic relief. My husband Bob likewise allowed me to use his actual witticisms and those I made up in my head, and suffered through the weekly rough draft readings.

The concept of Mombo would not have materialized without the guidance and skill of Daphne Backman of Ice-dance.com and the editing and graphic skills of Michelle Wojdyla. I was encouraged by the skaters and parents through the years, and kept on track by my biggest fan and critic, Melissa Hammond. A hundred thank yous could never really let them all know how much I appreciated their comments and words in response.

And thanks to the Corona family: John for being a fabulous skating partner, and Deanna, who always had the strength to watch the ice and give me the play-by-plays. One of the added benefits of the sport is that you meet people who become and remain family.

My final words of gratitude go to Melaney Moisan, my friend, my editor, and my publisher. When we walked into that tattoo parlor in Baltimore in 2001 to celebrate our MFA graduation, I had no idea we would continue sharing ink in the coming years, but what a great journey it has been.

And the journey continues, Thanks to all.

Author's Bio

Sherry Bosley holds an MFA in Creative Nonfiction from Goucher College. She has won several writing awards including one from *The Atlantic Monthly*. She writes an online blog for an Ice Dance website, contributes to *The Baltimore Sun* and *Salon.com*, and is featured in the anthology *New Lines from the Old Line State*. She lives in Bel Air, Maryland, with her husband, Bob; her son, Adam (when he's not in college); and ice-dancing daughter, Pilar (when she's not skating, coaching, or attending college); as well as the vivacious Miss Izzy, the feisty fox terrier, and Eliot, the stately standard poodle.

Photo by Karen Quatman